cyclosportive+

CHRIS SIDWELLS

cyclosp

ortive+

Preparing for and taking part in long-distance cycling challenges

While every effort has been made to ensure that the content of this book is as technically accurate and as sound as possible, neither the author nor the publishers can accept responsibility for any injury or loss sustained as a result of the use of this material.

Note: throughout the book, riders and officials are referred to as 'he'. This should, of course, be taken to mean 'he or she' where applicable.

Published in the UK in 2011 by
A&C Black Publishers Ltd an imprint of Bloomsbury Publishing Plc
36 Soho Square, London W1D 3QY
www.acblack.com

Copyright © Chris Sidwells 2011

ISBN 978 1 4081 4022 2

All rights reserved. No part of this publication may be reproduced in any form or by any means – graphic, electronic or mechanical, including photocopying, recording, taping or information storage and retrieval systems – without the prior permission in writing of the publishers.

Chris Sidwells asserted his right under the Copyright, Design and Patents Act, 1988, to be identified as the author of this work.

A CIP catalogue record for this book is available from the British Library.

Commissioned by Charlotte Croft
Edited by Rebecca Senior
Designed by Steve Russell
Cover photograph © Getty Images
Inside photographs p 6, 10, 11, 18, 50, 51, 67, 76, 110 © Getty Images; p 87, 104, 106, 107, 113, 114, 115, 116, 117, 131, 132, 133, 135 © Shutterstock; p 4, 5, 40, 69 © Gerard Brown; p 82 © Frazer Waller; p 103, 119 © Andy Jones; p 108 © Istock image bank. All other photographs © Chris Sidwells

This book is produced using paper that is made from wood grown in managed, sustainable forests. It is natural, renewable and recyclable. The logging and manufacturing processes conform to the environmental regulations of the country of origin.

Typeset by seagulls.net in 9pt Meta Plus

Printed and bound in China by C&C Offset Printing Co.

+ Contents

Foreword 1
Introduction 3
001 : **The Sportive World** 7
002 : **Getting Started** 19
003 : **Cyclosportive Skills** 41
004 : **Sportive Demands** 65
005 : **Sportive Training** 77
006 : **Sportive Nutrition** 105
007 : **Going Further** 121
008 : **Bike Care** 139

Useful References 155
Index 159

About the Author

Chris Sidwells is a freelance writer and photographer specialising in all aspects of cycling. His words and pictures appear in numerous magazines, including Britain's number one, *Cycling Weekly*. *Cyclosportive* is Chris's eighth cycling book, and a number of them have been best sellers. His titles range from biography to bike maintenance, and his work has been translated into twenty-four languages.

He is a lifelong cyclist and has won races in every discipline: road, track and off-road. He has also won in every age group, from youths to masters. In cyclosportive Chris achieved gold medal standard in the Etape du Tour. He is also a qualified cycling coach and a fitness instructor.

+ Foreword

Cycling has undergone a revolution during the last ten years: it has become fashionable. The bikes, the clothes and the lifestyle appeal to people in numbers never known before. What other form of exercise doubles as your ride to work and a vehicle to explore the countryside, and is always there for fun and adventures?

And you can use your bike to challenge yourself, or others, or the terrain; traditionally by racing, but more recently in a type of mass-participation event called a cyclosportive. These long-distance rides, often along challenging routes, have grown quickly to rival the incredible marathon-running boom of the 1980s.

They underline the very essence of cycling: that bikes allow people to travel long distances under their own power much faster then they could by using only their own two feet. Bikes are the definition of man, woman and machine working in harmony, as they roll over our planet leaving hardly a trace behind.

Cyclosportives are for everyone. You'll find them in all corners of the world. Taking part means anything you want it to mean, from completing the distance to setting the fastest time. You decide what that challenge is.

They're tough, just like running a marathon is tough – although, as with marathons, you set your own pace. And preparation pays dividends. That's where this book comes in. In it, I'll show you the most efficient way to meet the challenge and get what you want from cyclosportives. I'll tell you what bike to buy; how to set it up and look after it; and how to ride in a way that will enhance your enjoyment and help you achieve your goals. I'll look at how to train, what to eat and what to do in an event. So read on ... then hit the road, and get pedalling.

+ Introduction

What is a cyclosportive?

Cyclosportive: a modern long-distance cycling challenge

The word 'cyclosportive' is French, and the spirit of modern cyclosportive events is very European in that they mimic the physical challenge of professional bike racing, which is historically a Euro-centric sport. However, like professional cycling, cyclosportives have spread throughout the world. Some of the biggest mass participation sporting events on the planet are cyclosportives in South Africa, Australia and America. Wherever you live, the chances are you will be able to find an event to take part in.

A cyclosportive, or sportive as the name is often shortened to, is a cycle ride, usually with a choice of distances ranging from 50km (although they are rarely as short as that) to well over 200km. Some cyclosportives use the same roads as races known in cycling as *the classics*; others use routes devised by their organisers. The one thing they share, though, is the toughness of their routes.

Toughness is the challenge and the attraction of cyclosportive. The queen event, the Etape du Tour, is an actual stage of the Tour de France over which the pros race in the same year. Recently that stage has been in one of France's great mountain ranges – the Alps or the Pyrenees. Events in other countries are just as hard, just as classic.

Who rides cyclosportives?

Anyone – in fact that is part of their attraction. Completing a big sportive isn't easy: it requires training, good preparation and application, plus raw dogged determination on the day. However, the modern bicycle is a wonderful machine, which gives back all you put into it, and more. You might have to start with a shorter event than the Etape du Tour – in fact if you are new to cycling you must do that – but completing a big sportive is within the physical grasp of almost anyone.

How do I improve?

Finishing is one thing, finishing in a better time is another. Cyclosportives are first and foremost participation events: finishing is the goal, and a totally valid one.

Having said that, the events are often timed and many organisers publish a finishing list split into gender and age groups, giving everyone something to go for. This book is aimed at both sets of people: those who want to take part and finish their first cyclosportive, or their first classic event; and to those who want to post a better time and finish higher up the list.

What does this book cover?

+ What kind of bike to buy
+ How to set up your optimal riding position
+ How to care for your bike

Cyclosportive_

+ **Clothing and equipment**
+ **Training**
+ **Diet and nutrition**
+ **Cyclosportive skills and techniques**
+ **Where to begin**
+ **How to take it further**
+ **Physical and mental demands of an event**

Cyclosportive will tell you all you need to know before taking part in your first cyclosportives, and it will help your progress towards other goals in this exciting and challenging new cycling phenomenon.

Essentially, it shows you how to train to meet the demands of what will be a challenging and unforgettable event. Whether you're approaching your first sportive or hoping to improve your performance, this book will show you how to train, how to ride and how to get the best from yourself.

+ The Sportive World
[chapter : 001]

There are cyclosportive events all over the world. They have grown as bike racing has grown into a global sport, and now every continent has its big bike races and its classic cyclosportives.

They also grew as bikes became accepted as the ultimate fitness tool. People the world over have chosen cycling as their way to get fit in the 21st century. Bikes combine a human fascination with technology and speed, with a need to exercise and feel the wind in the face.

Bikes are also something that featured in our childhood, when there were no barriers, no limits to what we imagined we could do. Bikes represent the chance to feel like that again, and among the many reasons for training and taking part in cyclosportives a child-like, visceral indulgence is a very strong one.

But cyclosportives also represent a challenge, a chance to set personal goals that are as basic or demanding as you want them to be. No one else sets your challenges, as they often do in everyday life, especially at work. You set them, you decide, and your effort will determine whether you achieve them, no one else's.

That's one of the beauties of cyclosportives. They are long-distance cycling challenges, often over tough courses, so the first challenge they present is simply completing the ride. And a very worthy one it is too.

That is what the majority of the entrants will be trying to do. They come from all sorts of backgrounds; new cyclists, people who have been riding for years, ex- and current racers to absolute beginners. There are all sorts of age groups, from teenagers to pensioners, and women make up a significant proportion of most cyclosportive events.

There is no reason why you shouldn't choose one of the big international events as your first one, so long as you don't underestimate what is required. And that is quite a lot of training, a good level of fitness, and some long rides in your legs.

What follows is a taster of what an event will be like, but what's mentioned here is expanded in much greater depth later in the book.

What to expect

Whether you opt for a local event, which is probably the best bet for your first one, or a big international, entries will either be made through the post or online. Then you need to familiarise yourself with all the information the organisers provide.

You need to know exactly where and when you start, and what energy drinks and food will be provided on the route. Use the same snacks in training to get used to them, unless there is something else you'd rather use, then you have to ensure you can carry enough of it to last. We talk about sportive nutrition fully in chapter 6.

Familiarise yourself with the route – where the climbs are and where landmarks are that divide the route up into sections – so you know how far you've ridden and how far there is left to ride and how tough it will be. A cycle computer is great for keeping an eye on this. And pack enough clothes for any weather conditions. Never assume it will be warm in summer and cooler in spring and autumn; take enough clothing to cope with anything all year round.

Arrive at the event with enough time to park, register and prepare your bike. One hour at least for small events and two hours for big ones. The biggest cyclosportives often allow registration the day before the event, and with fields of several thousand it's a good idea to take advantage of that. You will also receive a timing transponder at registration; put this on your bike or wear it exactly where the organisers specify during the ride. You must have the transponder on when you cross the start line, otherwise your time won't be registered.

Check your bike over two days before the event and give it a clean, because a clean bike is a great morale booster. We'll show what checks to make later in the book. If anything is worn, replace it straightaway and check the bike over again once the new part is fitted. Take tools and spares such as tubes, tyres brake and gear cable to the event, and always carry a saddle bag with at least one inner tube, three tyre levers and a multi-tool in it.

The start

Once you are registered and your bike is ready go for a little ride on it to stretch your legs and

settle any nerves. You don't really need to warm up for cyclosportives as they are long events and you need to save energy, but getting your legs loosened up a bit will make the first few kilometres more comfortable.

In bigger events you line up at the start according to your race number, lowest at the front highest at the rear. That can mean you might cross the start line some minutes behind the front of the pack, but your time is taken from when you (or rather your timing transponder) cross the start line, so don't worry about it.

Use the first few kilometres to settle yourself down. These are often a bit of a scramble with lots going on around you. There will be riders passing you, and moving this way and that in front of you as they try to make progress. Try to ignore them until things settle down and get less crowded.

Events often start in towns, but you quickly get out on the open road. The field will have thinned out a little, so it's time to assess how you feel. How's your pace? If you feel good increase it a bit, but always err on the side of caution.

Management mode

Once settled in it's time to go into management mode. Enjoy the day, the experience and the scenery, but don't get carried away and forget to manage your ride. Managing means constantly analysing what you are doing, keeping track of how far to go, how you feel. Most importantly though, keep drinking and eating. Drink sips of liquid every 15 minutes at least and take a gel or something small but solid every half an hour. If you have a watch with an alarm you can set it to beep every 15 minutes to remind you.

Managing your ride also includes keeping your effort as constant as possible. Don't push too hard up the hills, but don't back off and freewheel too much on the descents either. Descents are speed for free, so take advantage of them. Pedalling on straight stretches of descents where the gradient is less steep can save a lot of time. And follow in the slipstream of others where you can. We explain how to do these things later on. Finally, in the last 10 per cent of the ride, if you can increase your pace do so.

Once you cross the line enjoy the moment, reflect on what you have done and congratulate yourself. You can analyse what you did right or wrong later. Your priority now is rehydrating and eating. Have a sugary drink as soon as you finish, follow that with something that contains carbohydrate and protein within an hour of stopping, and try to eat a main meal within three hours. Avoid too much alcohol that night and go to bed early.

What next?

You've done your first sportive, so where do you go from here? The simple answer is anywhere. Cyclosportive events are springing up all around the world, so no matter where you live there will be a classic cyclosportive event. From a stage of the Tour Down Under in Australia to the Cape Argus Cycle Tour in South Africa (the biggest cyclosportive in the world by the way, with more than 40,000 entrants) and to the Sea Otter Classic in America, almost every country has caught the sportive bug and events are increasing in number each year.

However, the home of cyclosportive is Europe, where the same type of events are often called Grand Fondos in Italy, or simply given a name, one particular to the geography of a region. That applies to other countries too, and sometimes a sportive will be named after a professional race or a famous racer or is associated with a local cycling celebrity.

Arguably the most prestigious event is the Etape du Tour, a stage of the Tour de France. The route for this changes each year, but it is always very demanding and since 2000 it has always been a mountain stage.

Running the Etape close in popularity is another France classic, La Marmotte. This is held each year on the same route. It takes in the Alpine climbs made famous by 100 years of the Tour de France: the Croix de Fer, Telegraphe and Galibier and it finishes on top of Alpe d'Huez.

Italy has the Maratona dles Dolomites in their Alps, and many others that use mountain climbs chosen from their biggest professional stage race, the Giro d'Italia. There are also events in the Italian lake district, down the spine of Italy and close to the Adriatic. The names of these races often celebrate their most famous pro riders, such as Fausto Coppi, Felice Gimondi and Marco Pantani. There are long-established events in Spain, such as the Quebrantahuesos, and in Belgium, Holland and Germany. Almost everywhere in Europe in fact.

Or perhaps cycling the same route as the pros do in their biggest single-day races, *the classics*, grabs you. There's the Tour of Flanders in Belgium. Each year it attracts more than 18,000 people who want to test themselves over the short, sharp-cobbled climbs where the pros have fought to win their version since 1913. You can also do the Paris–Roubaix in France, a version of Liège–Bastogne–Liège in Belgium, and Milan–San Remo and the Tour of Lombardy in Italy. Along with Flanders these races make up the five biggest professional single-day races in the world. They are called *the monuments*.

A cyclosportive story_

All the big European cyclosportives are tough, but some can be extremely tough. Take, for example, the Etape du Tour in 2000. The route was in Haute-Provence, from the town of Carpentras to the top of the mountain that dominates the region – the incredible, formidable Mont Ventoux.

The Ventoux is the diva of Tour de France mountain climbs; it has moods, wildly different ones, and for those riding the 2000 Etape the Ventoux was in a very bad mood indeed.

The ride was 150km long, not far by Tour de France standards, and the route had several climbs before the big one, but none was too difficult. On top of that the weather was pleasant. It was sunny, warm but not hot, and in a region where heat can be a problem that was appreciated.

But there was a reason why it wasn't hot, and that only became clear on Mont Ventoux. The mountain has its own climate, and on the day of the Etape its near 2000-metre peak was stuck in the jet stream of the Mistral. This ferocious wind blows down the Rhône valley, dragging freezing air from snowfields on top of the Alps with it. It hits the Ventoux summit with such force that the world record wind speed of 290km/h was once recorded here. And when the Mistral hits the Ventoux, the peak sucks it downwards and blasts it on to its southern slopes.

That's the way the 2000 Etape climbed. The moment the participants hit the Ventoux their day changed as they were hit by a 100km/h headwind. The temperature dropped, mist fell, it even began to snow at one point. Next morning one French paper's headline reporting on the Etape read 'Apocalypse'. Riders weaved, they climbed out of the saddle, some walked. Eventually the police had to stop the event and only 3500 of the 7000-plus starters made it to the top.

Are you ready for that? You will be once you've read this book.

Famous cyclosportives

UK

 Etape du Dales

Distance: 180km
Start/Finish: Grassington in Yorkshire
Route: Through the Yorkshire Dales
Takes place: Mid-May
Principle difficulties: The Buttertubs Pass and Tan Hill
Rider level: Experience of riding 260km in UK is recommended
Background info: Situated in the heart of a strong cycling region, the Etape du Dales attracts a varied field from very fit racers through older, experienced riders to relative newcomers. The weather is usually mild, so isn't too much of a factor, and you are never very far from an aid station if you get into difficulties. The route is hilly but not mountainous

 The Dragon Ride

Distance: Choice of three: 40km, 130km and 190km
Start/Finish: Bridgend area, South Wales
Route: From the Welsh valleys and into the Brecon Beacons, depending on the distance chosen
Takes place: Late June
Principle difficulties: The Bwlch and Rhigos climbs, plus the Brecon Beacons for the longer distance
Rider level: From first timers to experienced competitors, depending on distance. The longer distance requires respect and some experience of 160km-plus sportives
Background info: The weather is usually good, but the longer routes qualify as mountainous. There is more than 3000m of climbing on the 190km route, so it requires a step-up in fitness and preparation from the Etape du Dales

France

 Etape du Tour

Distance: Varies each year but was 180km in 2010
Start/Finish: Varies each year
Route: A stage of the Tour de France is chosen as the route for this cyclosportive. It's almost always a mountainous one. The Alps and Pyrenees are alternated roughly each year
Takes place: Mid-July
Principle difficulties: Major Alpine or Pyrenean climbs, plus the weather
Rider level: Newcomers to cyclosportive do try the Etape each year, but they often come unstuck. Most who've done both agree that the Etape is a lot harder than running a marathon. Cyclosportive or cycle racing experience is recommended. The Etape is often won by a pro racer
Background info: Weather can be a factor. European mountain ranges are hot in summer, but freak cold conditions can also be experienced

 La Marmotte

Distance: 174km
Start/Finish: Le Bourg d'Oisans/Alpe d'Huez
Route: A classic loop through the high French Alps
Takes place: Mid-July
Principle difficulties: Col de la Croix de Fer, Col du Galibier and Alpe d'Huez
Rider level: Only riders with mountainous cyclosportive experience should try La Marmotte
Background info: Although the Etape du Tour is the most famous cyclosportive in the world, La Marmotte, with 5000m of climbing over three of the most famous mountains in the Tour de France, is consistently harder. There is also a very difficult descent of La Croix de Fer down the Glandon pass. You really must know what you are doing there.

 L'Ardéchoise

Distance: 216km
Start/Finish: St-Félicien
Route: Mountainous by British standards but not by French. However, there is very little flat on this route. The French would call the climbs 'moyen montagne' (middling mountains), about half the height and length as an average Alp
Takes place: Mid-June
Principle difficulties: Col du Buisson
Rider level: All-comers. Apart from the main event a number of others are run using parts of this route to make up an extended weekend. Distances range from 66km to 268km
Background info: The Ardèche is on the western edge of the Massif Central, just across the Rhône valley from Provence, so conditions should be hot in June. With an average of 17,000 participants this is one of the biggest cyclosportives in Europe

Italy

Felice Gimondi

Distance: 166km
Start/Finish: Bergamo
Route: Taking place in the Italian lake district of Lombardy and based on the type of steep but not too long climbs found in the pro race the Tour of Lombardy, you face more than 2800 vertical metres. Interspersed with that are stunning views of the lakes from the tops of the climbs and the roads that link them
Takes place: May
Principle difficulties: The Selvino Pass
Rider level: Quite experienced. A lot of ex-pros do this one, many of them friends of the man it is named after
Background info: Felice Gimondi comes from Bergamo and was one of Italian bike racing's best riders. He won the Tour de France in 1965 and won the Tour of Italy several times. He was also world road race champion in 1973. He's still active on his bike and often rides the event himself

L'Eroica

Distance: 200km with two shorter options
Start/Finish: In the area of Sienna, Tuscany, but changes
Route: Much of it is on the strada-bianca or white roads of this part of Italy. These are compressed powdered limestone, and cover the region in a grid pattern linking valleys and running up and down the long valley floors and hill tops. The roads are dusty, rough and liberally interspersed with potholes. There are no mountains, but not much flat either
Takes place: October
Principle difficulties: The strada-bianca roads
Rider level: All-comers, attracted by the wide variety of distances on offer. However, for each distance more than half the route will be on the white roads
Background info: The theme is retro. White roads are part of this region's history, and with that in mind the original event was for vintage bikes and riders in retro kit, although you can ride l'Eroica on a modern bike wearing modern kit. The more retro the better in fact: it's not unusual to see a rider dressed in 1940s gear and riding a 1940s bike. L'Eroica is what bike racing used to look like in the middle of the 20th century. The fun element is also pushed a lot, with many feed stations offering local sausage, cheese and bread, as well as plenty of Chianti to wash them down

Maratona dles Dolomites

Distance: 138km or more, with two shorter options
Start/Finish: Corvara
Route: Each route takes in some of the mountain passes made famous by the Tour of Italy, including two classic climbs, the Passo Giau and Passo Pordoi. These are not as long as French Alpine climbs, but are steeper
Takes place: July
Principle difficulties: Up to eight Alpine passes including the Passo Pordoi and Passo Giau
Rider level: All-comers, but the longest route attracts a lot of off-duty pro racers, plus many ex-champions
Background info: This is arguably the biggest cyclosportive in Italy, and they love their bikes in Italy. It's hard, chaotic and exuberant, just like the country

Belgium

 Tour of Flanders

Distance: Choice of three: 50km, 140km and 265km
Start/Finish: Ninove/Merelbeke (the 265km version starts in Bruges)
Route: The shortest route is for mountain bikes and has a lot of off-road. The longest ride covers exactly the same route as the professional race of the same name. The 140km route takes in all of the climbs that make this race one of the most famous and recognisable classic bike races in the world. The hills are all in the second half of the pro race anyway
Takes place: April, the day before the pro Tour of Flanders
Principle difficulties: Cobbled climbs such as the Kwaremont, Koppenberg and the Muur van Geraardsbergen
Rider level: Some 17,000 or more take part each year, so there is a big spread of ability and fitness. The longest distance is a real challenge, so it's suitable only for experienced riders. Also they have to provide support vehicles for themselves because the ride takes them across a whole region. It's a very accessible event with a great atmosphere and much of the route is lined by cheering spectators who are there for the weekend to watch the pros race next day
Background info: The Tour of Flanders has a special place in the heart of what is the most bike-mad region on the planet. The race is decided on a series of cobbled hills situated on one ridge in east Flanders. They identify and define the race. The long-distance ride takes its time getting there, the 140km option gets stuck into the hills almost from the off. They are short, steep and the cobbles will rattle your teeth. This is a must-do event that you will keep coming back to. The atmosphere it generates is addictive

 Tilf–Bastogne–Tilf

Distance: Choice of three: 72.5km, 136.5km and 232.5km
Start/Finish: Tilf, a small village outside Liège
Route: All the routes go south into the Ardennes hills that define the pro race. These are much longer climbs than you find in the Tour of Flanders and are like the sort of hills you experience in Wales or Yorkshire – steep and often straight but at the most 2km or 3km long. The longest ride stays true to the pro's route, except that it doesn't enter Liège
Takes place: Early May
Principle difficulties: Long and very steep hills including Stokeu, Haute Levée and La Redoute
Rider level: Beginners can chose the shortest route, while hardened enthusiasts go for the long one. The middle route attracts the greatest number of entries. It fits into the category of a double challenge. It will stretch you and needs plenty of preparation, but it isn't as gruelling as the long ride or one of the big mountain cyclosportives
Background info: This event was established to honour Belgium's other great classic, and its oldest bike race, Liège–Bastogne–Liège. The race began in 1892, and Bastogne chosen as the turn-around point because that was as far as the officials could get on the train to check the competitors through and still return to Liège in time to see them finish

Holland

Amstel Gold

Distances: Choice of four: 50km, 100km, 150km and 250km
Start/Finish: Valkenburg
Route: Very hilly and very complicated. You might think Holland is flat, and it is, apart from a tiny region right in the south-east corner of the country. The hills are short and steep but for the longest route to take them all in there are a lot of twists and turns, and ducking and diving around back streets. The route is well signposted throughout.
Takes place: April
Principles difficulties: The hills of an area of Holland known as Little Switzerland, including the Cauberg
Rider level: This one literally does attract everyone, from people riding Dutch sit-up-and-beg-type bikes doing the 50km ride to the really experienced on top-of-the-range racers testing themselves over 250km
Background info: This is another cyclosportive that follows a classic race route. The Amstel Gold Race is Holland's biggest pro race, and its succession of hills are a real challenge. Amstel is a brewery by the way, so post-ride refuelling traditionally involves beer.

Spain

Quebrantahuesos

Distance: 205km
Start/Finish: Sabiñánigo
Route: Enters the Pyrenees from the Spanish side, crosses to the French and returns, taking in three major mountain passes that have been ridden in the Tour de France and the Tour of Spain: Somport, Marie-Blanque and El Portalet. The last returns the route to Spain, where there are still two more big climbs before the finish
Takes place: June
Principles difficulties: Pyrenean climbs used in the Tour de France, including the Col de Somport, El Portalet and the Col de Marie-Blanque
Rider level: There is only one route and it is a big challenge, only for the experienced and fit. The route climbs the west side of the Marie-Blanque, the last 3km of which have a constant 12 per cent gradient
Background info: Quebrantahuesos are huge eagles that live in this part of the Pyrenees. You will see them on the ride, spiralling up on thermals in the air

Have these events whet your appetite? There are many, many more in the UK, throughout Europe and the world. At the back of the book we've listed some websites that provide details of how to enter some cyclosportive events. Many of the websites contain guides to the events and some include participants' experiences, which are often very helpful.

Most of the events listed are over one day, but an increasing number of multi-day cyclosportives are appearing. One example is the London to Paris, which is held in June over three days. This is billed as a pro event for amateur racers and has full back-up and an unusual format, where individual entrants compete as teams over certain stretches of each stage.

Whatever you chose to do, cyclosportive is a great way of enjoying your bike in the company of like-minded people and seeing different parts of the world at the same time. The events are a great introduction to the sport of bike racing too, as well as a way of experiencing the unique cycling culture in different countries.

Cyclosportives are where sport cycling and cycling for leisure merge into one big enjoyable movement. Try one and you'll be hooked and quickly ticking others off like badges of honour.

+ Getting Started
[chapter : 002]

This section looks at what sort of bike and what extras you need to buy, plus clothing for summer and winter riding. It covers setting up your bike, which is really important for your comfort as well as enabling you to get optimum power into the pedals while being as aerodynamic as possible. Having the correct bike set-up will help prevent injuries. Because we are all different, it's crucial that you get your personal bike set-up just right.

You don't have to copy what pro bike racers ride in terms of equipment, but you need to copy the way they personalise their bike set-up.

What bike do I need?

You could take part in a sportive on a hybrid bike – a cross between a road and mountain bike – or even a mountain bike fitted with slick tyres, but it

What's the difference?_

Road bikes are fitted with derailleur gears. These shift the chain between chainrings attached to the pedals, and sprockets on the rear wheel. Gear ratios depend on which chainring is driving which sprocket. A large chainring driving a small sprocket gives a high ratio, a small chainring driving a large sprocket means a low ratio.

But because cyclosportives are long and often hilly, cyclosportive bikes are fitted with smaller chainrings, often called a compact chainset, and a wider size-range of sprockets than you find on road race bikes. This preserves some high ratios but gives more low ratio gears to choose from, including very low ones. That allows you to conserve energy when climbing. Being economical with your energy is one of the keys to success

in the long-distance cycling challenge of cyclosportives.

The length and hilly nature of sportive courses means you will spend a relatively long time on your bikes during an event. This places a lot of strain on your back, shoulder and neck muscles, so cyclosportive bikes are made a little shorter and a little higher at the front to offer the option of a less stretched-out riding position. At the same time though you can still use the bottom of the dropped handlebars to create a lower and therefore more aerodynamic position on the faster parts of the course. Swapping positions to make the best of a course is another key factor in sportives. It's part of a philosophy that will reoccur throughout this book, and that's speed for free. Being aerodynamic requires no extra input of energy from you, but you end up riding faster, so it's speed for free.

Cyclosportive_

would make doing so a lot harder than it should be. What you really need is the sort of bike racers use for road racing – or even better a road race bike that has been designed specifically for the demands of cyclosportive events.

Road race bikes – or road bikes as they are more commonly known – are light. They have narrow, smooth tyres that roll easily along the road but still grip in the corners. They also have dropped handlebars, which you can hold in several positions. Hold them at the bottom for an aerodynamic position while travelling fast on the flat or downhill; or sit higher, grip the tops of the handlebars, or the brake levers, and pull harder with your arms when riding uphill.

Cyclosportive-specific road bikes are just as light as their similarly priced race equivalents. They have the same narrow tyres and dropped handlebars, but they have two major modifications to the basic road bike design that make them more suitable for sportive events:

+ a wider and lower range of gear ratios than road bikes;
+ a shorter reach to reduce stress on back, shoulder and neck muscles.

Bike materials

You can get a good cyclosportive bike, such as the Verenti Kilmeston, for around £900. It has an aluminium frame with carbon-fibre forks, a great combination as aluminium is light and stiff, so it minimises any flex in the frame that will soak up some of your valuable energy. Carbon fibre helps absorb road vibrations to increase riding comfort and control. The bike is equipped with a compact chainset and a wide range of sprockets. The geometry and dimensions of this bike's frame will allow you to ride for hours without overly tiring your neck, shoulder and back muscles.

+ The Verenti Kilmeston

20

+ The Boardman 9.2

It's a perfect bike for cyclosportives, and could be the only bike you will ever need. However, if you really get hooked on taking part in sportives and would like to improve your time for a certain course, or even get competitive within your age group, then there are bikes that are a little more technically advanced. They are also a little more expensive.

What you are paying extra for are the lighter materials used to manufacture these bikes. As you'll see later in this book, weight is a big issue in cycling. In fact the crucial equation that expresses cycling ability is the amount of power a person can produce divided by their weight and the weight of their bike. Any weight that can be saved translates into increased speed and a better performance. The expense comes when making light materials as strong and resilient as heavier ones. A lot of design thought and research and development go into that, and it's these you are paying for. It's speed for free in terms of energy, although in the case of lighter bikes, not in terms of money.

There are a lot of top cyclosportive-specific bikes on the market, and many have similar geometry to the Verenti Kilmeston but are a great deal lighter. If you are new to cycling or have any back issues they are the sort of bike I'd recommend you buy. However, if your ambition is to do faster times and finish higher up the field then a bike such as the Boardman 9.2 (see above) would be a good choice. Its frame is made from custom-specified carbon fibre. Not only is this lighter than aluminium but it also absorbs road vibrations better, and the carbon fibres are oriented in different ways throughout the frame to optimise their properties, which accounts for some of its price. This means that the bike has a comfortable frame that resists flex, but is considerably lighter than aluminium.

This bike is fitted with a standard road race chainset, which could easily be swapped for a compact. As it is pictured here it mimics the riding position of a standard cyclosportive bike by having several spacers on the steering tube, arranged underneath the handlebar stem. However, the thing with this bike is that as you get faster you can lower the handlebars by swapping these spacers, one or more at a time, and placing them above the stem. This will make your riding position more aerodynamic, which in turn makes you faster.

The Boardman 9.4 bike has lighter equipment than the basic bike, particularly the wheels and tyres. A bike such as this could cost more than £3000, although models that are aimed at the same kind of rider start at less than £1500.

Adaptations for winter

If you are new to cyclosportives then a good reason for choosing a bike like the Verenti Kilmeston is its adaptability. You can use it in the summer then add some extra equipment to it to make your winter rides more comfortable.

How to protect yourself and your bike

+ Fit mudguards to it.
+ Fit wider and heavier tyres to help ward off punctures.
+ Fit lights. Even if you never ride in the dark, small LED lights fitted to the front and rear of your bike make you more visible to other road users on gloomy days.
+ Wash it after every wet ride (we'll show you a quick, efficient way of doing this in chapter 8, Bike Care).

+ The Verenti Klimeston, with mudguards and lights fitted

Top cyclists say that medals are actually won during the winter, they are only awarded in summer. The same is true to a certain extent for someone taking part in sportives. Preserving and even building on your summer fitness during the winter will bring your sportive ambitions closer, but winter cycling can be a problem due to the cold and rain.

Not only does this make you less likely to put in the training you need but also rainwater corrodes your bike, especially when mixed with the salt they spread on roads when it's icy. Punctures can be a problem in winter too, because grit and glass gets washed on to the roads. Also the days are short and even in broad daylight you can end up riding in murky conditions.

Bikes such as this Verenti Klimeston are designed to take full mudguards and wider tyres. You can fit LED lights to any bike. If you start with a bike such as this one, you can update to a lighter more expensive one later if you wish, then keep this bike for training, especially during the winter. If you start out with an expensive bike and don't want to buy a cheaper one just for winter training, then buying some training wheels with heavier tyres, plus a short mudguard called a spray guard, will make your bike good for winter rides. You will need to lavish extra care on it though, as really light equipment is sometimes not as robust as heavier stuff.

+ Bottles and a bottle cage

Other bike essentials:

+ Drinks bottles and bottle cages
+ Multi-tool
+ Spare inner tube, tyre levers, and pump or other inflator
+ Under-the-saddle bag

Why you need these bike essentials

Drinks bottles and bottle cages

Keeping well hydrated is crucial when exercising, your performance level drops if you don't. Getting dehydrated can even be dangerous. Cyclists drink from bottles designed to be carried on their bikes in holders called bottle cages, which are bolted to

the frame's down tube and seat tube. There are a wide range of cages on the market, and expensive ones aren't necessarily the best. Go for straightforward designs such as the one pictured on page 23.

Multi-tool

Multi-tools are like Swiss Army knives for cyclists. They have a body like a penknife out of which various tools, such as screwdrivers and Allen keys, can be drawn to tackle straightforward adjustments, tighten something up or make simple repairs.

+ The essential multi-tool

Spare inner tube, tyre levers, and pump or other inflator

You will have punctures, they are a fact of cycling life. And when you do it's quicker and easier to replace the inner tube with a good one then repair the punctured one at home, which becomes your new spare. You need tyre levers to remove and replace the tyre. There are gas canisters to inflate tyres, even some that inject a sealant into the inner tube for an on-the-spot repair, but hand pumps are tried and tested. Buy a small hand pump that inflates with both in and out strokes.

+ An inner tube, tyre lever and pump

+ A GPS fitted on the handlebars

Under-the-saddle bag

Keep your spare tube, tyre levers and multi-tool, plus some money for emergencies, in a bag that clips or straps under your saddle. Very small pumps can go in the bag too. However, you should wrap these things in individual pieces of cling film to prevent damage caused when they rub together. Larger pumps should be fitted on to the frame, and most come with attachments to do this. Don't carry pumps or other spares in your pockets as they take up valuable space, they get in the way and they can bounce out.

Kit also worth having:

+ Cycle computer
+ GPS
+ Heart-rate monitor
+ Lights
+ Mudguards
+ Turbo trainer

What to buy

Cycle computers

Cycling lends itself to numbers, and numbers can help give direction to your training. Numbers are something you can work on, you can add to or subtract from them. Numbers bring control and provide encouragement.

It's nice to know how far you have ridden, and if you are riding further in the same time as you progress it spurs you on. Cycle computers provide information like that, plus they record your average speed, and some even tell you how many metres or feet you've climbed during a ride.

GPS

These are great for trying out new riding routes. You just decide where you want to go from a computer map, download the chosen route and follow it on

Cyclosportive_

+ A heart-rate monitor

the handlebar-mounted screen. There are models that can record valuable training information too.

Heart-rate monitors

These are a brilliant aid to your training in that they give you precise control of the effort you are making. They also help you map improvements. However, you need to be quite rigorous in the way you use them. We'll look at heart-rate monitors in detail in the training section of the book.

+ LED lights front and back

Lights

LED lights are small and can be used in flashing or constant mode. A red LED on the rear and white on the front of any bike will make you more visible to other road users. If you ride at night then such lights are required by law. You can have as many of each as you like. LEDs, one of which should be on constant mode, are best at the rear. There's a wide variety of front lights, but go for the most powerful you can afford. These often come with separate rechargeable battery packs, such as the one pictured, and as well as being seen they allow you to see where you are going in pitch darkness.

Mudguards

There are two types of mudguards: those that attach to threaded fastenings on the bike frame, and those that have their own fastenings. The latter are designed to fit race or top-end cyclosportive bikes. Top-end bikes don't have the threaded fastenings on their frames that the Verenti has, and their frames have only enough space for the tyres to fit. This makes them more responsive, so faster, but the only mudguards you can fit to these bikes are ones with their own attachments, and even then the job can be fiddly. A spray guard that clips on to the seat post of your bike is another mudguard option.

+ A clip-on mudguard

> **Cycling fact_**
> Think of drag as a force resisting you riding forwards. The relationship between a cyclist and drag is roughly this: if you double your speed, the force of drag quadruples. This is a very important fact of cycling and we'll refer to it constantly throughout this book.

Turbo trainer

We're inclined to put a turbo trainer in with bike essentials. Buy one, embrace what it can do for you and it will become your best friend when training for cyclosportives. Turbo trainers have two functions: you can train indoors when the weather or light conditions would make training outdoors uncomfortable or dangerous; and they bring a precision to your training that is hard to mimic outdoors. We'll talk about turbo trainers later on and into why that precision is important for some aspects of your training.

Go for a turbo trainer with fan resistance, as these mimic the effects of riding outside. With a fan turbo trainer, the harder you pedal the faster your back wheel revolves a fan that is part of the trainer. The fan is designed to scoop up air, and any object passing through air creates drag. So, since drag increases at the square of speed, if you pedal harder the fan creates proportionately more drag for you to overcome. This mimics what it's like to ride along the road. As you go faster the drag you create increases at a faster rate than your speed, so it becomes harder and harder to keep increasing your speed. Eventually drag becomes a limiting factor on how fast you can ride.

In addition to the fan, the turbo may also have other ways of increasing resistance, such as by using magnetic forces, which is good, because you can mimic the effects of hills like this. Some turbo trainers have fans that run in liquid instead of air, which is fine because drag in liquids is very similar to drag in air. The faster you go the harder it gets to increase speed.

It's good to have something to listen to or watch when riding on a turbo trainer, like your favourite music on an MP3 player or you could watch a DVD. A turbo trainer's biggest drawback is that it turns your bike into a piece of exercise machinery. That's not what bikes are about at all, but stick with this aspect of your training because it pays back in spades.

Clothing

What to wear in summer

Always start with a base layer made from a 'wicking' material, a thin one for summer. Thicker 'wicking' base layers are available for winter riding.

+ On warm days

Wear bib shorts and a short-sleeved top over the base layer. Lycra shorts 'wick' sweat away, and their tight fit prevents chaffing and makes them aerodynamic. Tops should fit fairly closely for the same reasons. Cycling shorts are padded where you sit on the saddle to provide a layer of cushioning and further reduce chaffing. Check the stitching in this area to ensure it's flat and unobtrusive before buying. If you are trying on shorts in a shop, remember to bend over to see if they will be comfortable when you are riding.

Cycling tops have pockets on their backs to carry food. Full-zipped tops are best for summer as you can pull them right down to let the air circulate around you when it's hot. Don't forget to zip them back up on descents to prevent getting too cold or even catching a chill. Zipped-up tops improve aerodynamics too, which will increase your average

> **Cycling fact_**
> Wicking materials absorb body perspiration and pass it to their surface where it evaporates. Cyclists wear them next to the skin because they help to keep it dry, reducing discomfort and the chilling effect of the wind.

+ Warm-weather clothing

speed and lower your finish time. Remember, zipping up your top equals speed for free.

Helmets are essential. Buy one that suits you. That's important because if you aren't happy you won't wear it for every ride, and you should do that. Ask for help in the shop if you aren't sure about the fit. It shouldn't pinch you but should fit close enough to your head so that it moves your scalp when you move the helmet. Look for a model with lots of ventilation. Modern bike helmets are so light and so well designed that after a while you won't notice you've got one on.

Short-fingered gloves called track mitts absorb sweat and give you a good grip on your handlebars. They prevent chaffing and can be invaluable in a fall, when you tend to put your hand out and so can suffer cuts and grazes. Track mitts greatly reduce such injuries.

Cycling shoes have stiff soles, so all your leg power gets transferred to the pedals, and breathable uppers. Make sure they are compatible with your pedals. I recommend you use clipless pedals for cyclosportives. These work by means of a cleat attached to each shoe sole, which engages with a retaining device on the pedals. Once you 'click' your foot into the pedal you are attached to your bike. So again, all your power goes into turning the pedals. A simple sideways twist of your foot releases it.

Cycling fact_
Why bib shorts and not just shorts? Bib shorts have high backs and loops that go over your shoulders to ensure a good fit and to cover your lower back when you bend into a crouched riding position. This stops back muscles getting chilled on descents or if the temperature is low or it rains. Chilled muscle tissue contracts, and if the big muscles in your lower back start doing that on long bike rides you will get back problems.

Finally, wear cycling-specific socks. They are thinner than running socks and wick sweat away from your feet.

+ On chilly summer days

Arm warmers and leg warmers are extensions to your shorts and top that you can add or remove whenever you wish. They should fit closely but comfortably. When you buy look for 'grippers' around the top. These hold the warmers in place, preventing them moving down your arm or leg as you ride along.

A gilet is a thin, sleeveless body warmer with a full zip. It should fold up small enough to stuff in a jersey pocket if the weather gets warmer. Another good top to have for summer and winter is a full-sleeved waterproof top. Buy a cycling-specific one though.

And that completes your summer wardrobe.

What to wear in winter

Again, start with a wicking base layer, thicker than summer if the temperature is low. Bib tights are next, these are just long versions of bib shorts. They are made from a fleecy kind of lycra. The light fleece is inside, next to the skin, so micro-air pockets in the fleece help retain your body heat. Don't be tempted to buy really thick bib tights, unless you live somewhere very cold. On top of the bib tights and your base layer you can wear a winter cycling jacket, or a mid-layer plus a thinner outer windproof top. Add or subtract tops to suit the temperature.

Avoid bib tights with extra padding or thickness in the knee area. The idea of this is to keep your knees warm, but in fact the extra thickness can push your kneecap out of line and cause knee problems.

Thermal socks are a must for winter cycling, plus overshoes. Overshoes are made from a number of materials, such as neoprene. They stretch over your cycling shoes and stop the cold getting to your feet.

+ To keep the summer chill off

Cyclosportive_

+ Winter clothing

+ Overshoes

You'll build up your experience of what works, but we recommend buying two thermal base layers, some bib tights, a thin winter top, plus a heavier winter cycling top. Add in the gilet you use on chilly spring, summer or autumn days and your waterproof top and you have a good cycling wardrobe. Your short-sleeved summer tops make good alternative mid-layers. And on mild winter days you can wear your bib shorts and leg warmers.

Kit fine print

Some extra bits and bobs you'll need:

+ Chamois crème
+ Lip salve
+ Protective body oils
+ Sunscreen
+ Wind chill table

Chamois crème is a lubricant that can be applied to the protective pad inside cycling shorts. Its name comes from the fact that years ago these pads were made from real chamois leather, which required softening after washing. Most pads are synthetic chamois now, and don't require anything to soften them. However, if you have a tendency to suffer from saddle soreness or chaffing, and some people do – even Tour de France pros – then chamois crème could be the answer. Don't underestimate saddle soreness – it can be a showstopper in a long sportive, and in any case it's very uncomfortable.

When training in cold dry conditions, or when wind chill is a factor, lip salves help prevent your lips cracking. Smear a layer on your lips before setting off, and it should be enough to protect you from what can be a painful experience.

Protective body oils are useful in cold and wet conditions. Often lanolin based, when rubbed on your legs, back and arms they can help preserve body heat by providing a barrier against cold water. Some cyclists prefer to coat their legs with such products instead of wearing leg warmers in cyclosportives or races run off in cold conditions.

You need protection from the sun, even on dull days, in hot countries and in mountainous terrain.

> **Tip_ The need for layers**
> Layering is a technique to combat cold by wearing several thin layers instead of one or two thick ones. The idea is that air is trapped between the layers, which the body heats, and that helps to keep you warm. Nowadays though single pieces of clothing, in particular some winter cycling tops, possess the same characteristics of several layers in one garment. That's why a thermal base layer and a winter-specific top work just fine in all but the coldest conditions.

Also you need it all the time when the sun is out during the summer in more temperate zones. Nowadays you can buy sunscreens designed specifically for sport. Check the label: the sunscreen should protect against UVA and UVB light, contain a stabiliser so you don't have to reapply them often, and be sweat resistant. Apply sunscreen 30 minutes before exposure so it soaks into your skin, because that makes it more effective. And put plenty on.

Wind chill is where the speed of the wind effectively lowers air temperature. It's a bigger factor at low temperatures than high ones, so it's significant in winter. Wind chill can lower the temperature to a point where frostbite can occur in exposed skin, even in the UK. Many clothing manufacturers produce wind chill tables, and you can get one by searching online. Wind chill has a great bearing on whether a training session is best done outside or indoors. Remember too that wind chill can be significant at altitude, even in summer, when it can be sweltering hot at the bottom of an Alpine pass, but just above zero at the top.

Bike set-up

You are the engine that powers your bike, but an engine can only provide the power it's capable of if it is mounted correctly. It's the same for you, your power is transferred to your bike through a series of levers: primarily your legs, but your arms, shoulders, back and mid-section come into play as well.

The first step in getting your levers working optimally is buying the correct size of bike. It pays to take advice from a reputable bike shop, or get a coach or even an experienced cyclist to help you with this. Once you have the bike though, you need to custom fit it to your body. This is done by altering the height and position of your saddle relative to the bike pedals. Once this is established you look at the position of your handlebars relative to the saddle.

There are a number of bike shops and coaches who specialise in bike fitting. We've asked a former Tour de France finisher, who is now a coach, Adrian Timmis, to illustrate how he fits a customer to a bike. If you follow this step-by-step guide your bike set-up should be near perfect. You'll need someone to help you with parts of it though.

Step 01

Start with your feet, which are a crucial although often overlooked part of getting power to your pedals. They are the last link with the pedals, so foot position is the first thing you must get right before setting anything else up. You must therefore have the cleats on your shoes positioned correctly so that you transfer maximum power when the widest part of your foot, or the ball of the foot as it is also known, is directly over the pedal axle. To ensure this, put your cycling shoes on and mark the position where your foot is widest on the outside of each shoe.

Engage the cleats with each pedal and get the person assisting you to note if the mark on your shoes is in front, behind or dead level with each pedal axle. If it's in front or behind loosen the cleat fixings and move the cleat into line. Most cleats have a centre line marked on them, so just line that up with the mark you made on the outside of each shoe.

Step 02

Take off your shoes and measure your inseam. That's the distance from your crotch to the floor when your leg is straight. Multiply this figure by 0.833 and set your saddle height, that's the distance from the top of the saddle down the seat tube to the centre of the bike's bottom bracket, to the resulting figure plus 0.5cm. For example, if your inseam is 79cm, the saddle height you set initially will be 79x0.833 = 65.81cm (+ 0.5cm) = 66.3cm.

Place your bike on a turbo trainer. If you haven't got one, or can't get hold of one, just go with the 0.883 of inseam, don't add the 0.5cm, because that's so you can do some fine tuning and only works with a turbo. Once on the turbo begin pedalling and listen to the noise the turbo makes. If it is a constant noise then your saddle height is correct, but if it comes and goes in a whoosh whoosh noise it's too high. Lower it by 2mm at a time until the turbo noise becomes more constant.

Timmis says: 'You are looking for a Eureka moment when the pedalling sounds right. That sound is feedback to indicate when you are applying most power. When the sound is nearest constant you are applying power through most of each pedal revolution.'

Cyclosportive_

Step 03

The final step in getting your main lever, your legs, into the perfect position for optimal power transfer is to set up your saddle set-back. This is the position your saddle is fixed in relative to an imaginary line drawn vertically up from your bike's forward pedal axle when the bike's cranks are parallel to the floor.

Timmis uses a laser beam for this step, but you can use a builder's plumbline. Pedal for a while so you are settled and your sit bones are in the most comfortable place on your saddle. Stop with your cranks parallel to the floor and get your assistant to drop the plumb-line from the hollow just behind your knee cap and to the outside of your leg. The weighted end should drop directly on to the mark you made on the outsides of your shoes, which are now both over each pedal axle. If it doesn't, undo the saddle fixing bolt(s) and move your saddle forwards or backwards until it does.

Step 04

Once your feet and saddle are in the right position relative to the pedals, it's time to look at your other point of contact with your bike, the handlebars. Handlebar stems rarely need changing as they increase in size relative to the size of bike you buy. To test if yours is right put your hands on the bottom of the handlebars while you are riding. If the front hub is hidden by your handlebars the stem is the correct length. If you see the hub in front of the handlebars the stem is too short; if it's behind, the stem is too long. If either of these is the case you need a different stem.

At the same time, if you feel constricted when holding the bottom of the handlebars you might also need a different kind of stem to raise your handlebars, or it might be possible to swap spacers on the steerer to do this.

If the stem is the correct length and you don't feel constricted then remove the handlebar tape before setting your brake levers and handlebars to the correct position. The bottom, straight section of your handlebars should be parallel with the floor, so when you hold the bottoms your hands are in line with your forearms. Adjust the handlebars until this is so.

To set your brake levers correctly, loosen the fixing bolts so that they can move on the handlebars. With your bike on a turbo trainer, get on it and ride with your eyes shut while holding the tops of the brake levers. Move the levers up and down on the handlebars until you feel most comfortable. Get off your bike, check the levers are level with each other on the handlebars and tighten up the fixing bolts again.

With your bike set up it's time to start riding with an eye on your first event, but what's on offer in the world of cyclosportives? Read the next chapter to find out.

Case Study

First-time participant: Jo Dytch

My first cyclosportive was a women-only event called the Diva 100 in Sussex. There were two distances, 50 and 100 kilometres, so being almost a novice cyclist I decided to ride the 50. I work in sports promotion and have worked on cyclosportives, which is why I wanted to take part in one. I'd seen how much fun they are and really enjoyed being with the people who take part in them.

I've always been fairly sporty and I like to keep myself fit. I run and have done some low-key triathlons, but I had had very little cycling experience before I entered the Diva. They are long-distance rides so I thought it was important to do the distance in training, or at least get close to it. So my key training sessions in the month or so leading up to the event were rides of 30 miles, which were actually a bit much for the first one, then 23, 28 and finally 30 miles. I spread these rides a week apart and in between time I cycled to work and back, did some running and my normal fitness stuff, as well as some shorter bike rides.

I did the long rides with my father, who's an experienced cyclist, and I think that helped. It also helped being in a women-only event. It can be quite intimidating when you are surrounded by men who look like they know what they are doing and you don't.

However, I have found that cyclists are very friendly and approachable. If you ask they will help you. I switched to using clipless pedals recently and was really worried about getting my feet in and out of them, but with a bit of advice I soon got used to them and can see why they are better.

You don't need to be super fit to do the sort of sportive I did, but riding for 50 kilometres felt good and it has made me want to do more – a lot more in fact. I'm going to try some longer sportives now and one day I'd like to do the Etape du Tour.

The other good thing I've discovered about cycling is the joy of riding in the countryside. If you do the long bike rides you need to do for sportives in nice surroundings, they don't seem like training, they're just fun rides. And if you can do them with a friend, they are even better.

I'd also recommend anyone to commute on their bike if they can. It gets you riding and some of the skills you learn from getting around cities on your bike are really helpful. I time my commute so that I'm not in the worst traffic, but it's still in central London, so it's busy. You have to be quite forceful, making definite signals and manoeuvres. If you are timid and stick to the inside of the road all the time, other drivers won't see you.

My commute isn't long so I wear ordinary clothes for it, but I always wear a helmet. For anything longer than my commute, I wear proper cycling stuff. I have two bikes, one for commuting and one for longer rides, training and sportives.

It's not a super-light racing bike, just a good dependable one with an aluminium frame. Looking after it and getting to know how it works was totally new, but again, other cyclists have helped, so has the shop I bought it from.

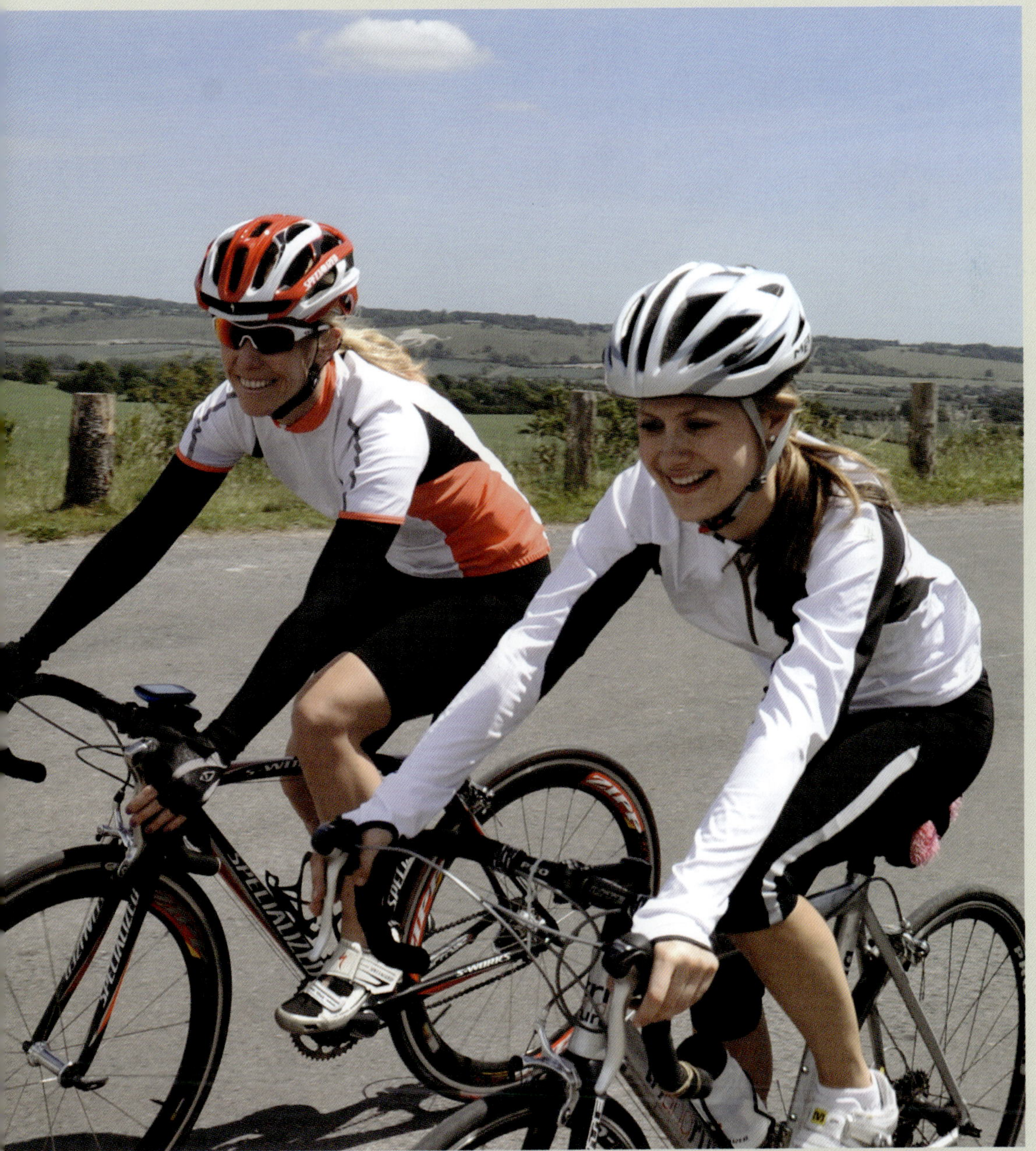

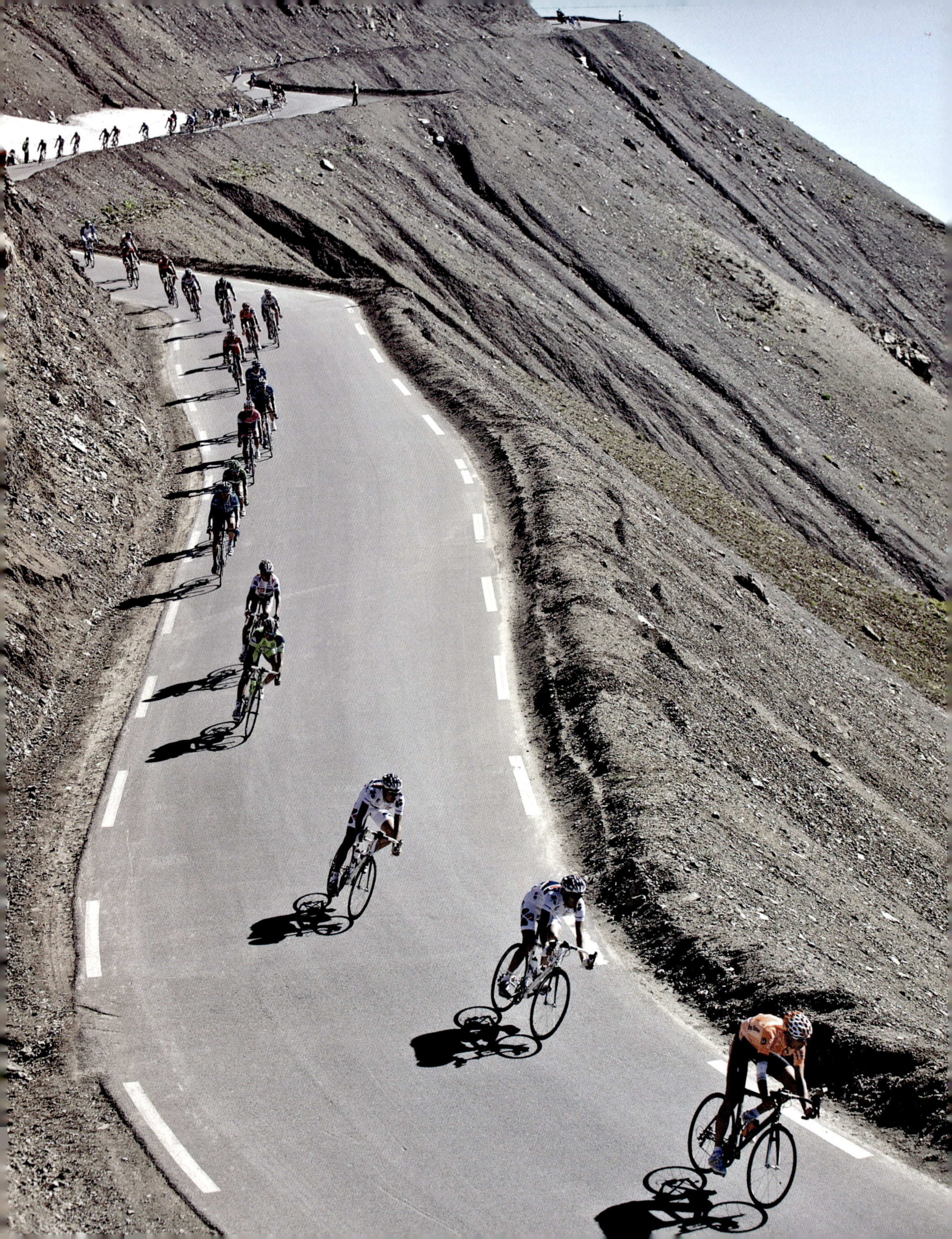

+ Cyclosportive Skills
[chapter : 003]

Success in cyclosportive is more certain if you master its core skills. They are all essential factors in helping you complete your first sportive, but within each one there are also more advanced modes that will help you progress. In addition you need to train to get as physically fit as you can, but that subject is so big it gets its own chapter – chapter 5 (Sportive Training).

The core skills are:

+ Pace judgement
+ Efficiency
+ Bike handling
+ Climbing
+ Group riding
+ Descending
+ Eating and drinking on your bike

Linked skills

Don't think of the skills as separate units, because they aren't – they are all linked. For example, good pace judgement over the whole duration of a sportive is a key to success, but pace judgement is crucial when climbing each individual hill. Good bike handling helps you ride well in a group, plus it helps you to speed down descents and through corners. Mastering every skill involves using elements of another skill, which is why they should be practised together if possible or at least in equal parts.

Pace judgement

Most of the skills required for success in cyclosportives are similar to those a road racer must master, except in one important aspect – pace judgement. To win or be placed high up in a road race you have to stay near the front. Breakaway groups can get a lead, but you must keep that lead within bounds and have the ability to pull it back, or get with it. To do that it's necessary at crucial stages of the race to push incredibly hard, harder than you would think is efficient in the long run, but if you don't there won't be a long run. You, or the group you are in, get left behind by the leaders and often there is no way back in a road race.

> **Tip_ Speed for free**
> This is a recurring philosophy throughout this book. Speed for free should be your cyclosportive mantra. It means taking advantage of anything that will increase your average speed, and therefore lower the total time you take to compete the event. Speed for free involves always being as aerodynamic as possible, taking advantage of fast descents, not braking too hard for corners and carrying speed through them. Even sheltering behind other riders, so not making as much effort as them, is part of speed for free.

+ Efficient cornering is speed for free

There are a lot of complicated reasons for this, mostly to do with the effects of drafting and the dynamics of road racing. Teamwork also plays a part in higher-level road races, where the objective is to ensure one or more members of a team is in a position to win at the end. But by and large these facets of road racing don't exist in cyclosportives, although some of them have their place if you want to finish high in your age group or do an excellent time.

But when you start out in sportives you can safely let riders go ahead in the knowledge that if you pace yourself more efficiently you could well catch them up later.

Case history: Alastair Kay_

Kay is from York and the top British finisher in the 2009 Etape du Tour. He explains his successful game plan: 'I'm an experienced road racer, but I didn't ride the Etape like a road race, whereas some other road racers I know did. It's a long day in the saddle, and the 2009 Etape finished with a climb of Mont Ventoux.

'The pace at the front was hard early on but I backed off from it because I wanted to save something for the Ventoux. I reckoned that's where the most time could be gained or lost. A pro racer I know went with the front riders right from the start, but he blew up and climbed the Ventoux in 1 hour 40 minutes, where I did it in 1 hour 20 and passed him, beating him by quite a bit.'

Tip_ Visualisation

To help you gain experience in riding sportives and get a better feel for what kind of effort you can support over a given length of time, visualise your energy as a big block in the middle of your body. The idea is to chip bits off this block until it is reduced to nothing by the end of the event, but only at the end of the event. Go too hard too early and the block will be gone before the end, leaving you exhausted and feeling as though you are a long way from home.

Kay (see box opposite) achieved his result because of pace judgement and good cycling efficiency that he's built over years of training, as well as bike handling skills he honed in road racing, and he is a very good climber.

But how do you judge what pace to ride a sportive at? Primarily it depends on how experienced and fit you are. The general rule is caution, start at a pace that feels within your capabilities and build on that. Ride within yourself on the hills, only pushing very hard on the final one or two. If you overdo it on an early climb you will pay for it later.

In chapter 5 (Sportive Training) we'll talk about levels of effort. Different systems work in your body at different levels of effort. Understanding them will help you judge the correct pace, but for now just bear in mind that if it hurts you are overdoing it.

Finishing a cyclosportive requires a lot of effort. You will breathe hard, you will experience discomfort. But when breathing hard crosses into being out of breath, when discomfort crosses into pain, you are riding too fast.

And remember the 'speed for free' mantra. Learn the skills and little bits of discipline involved, like doing up zips to prevent your top billowing out on descents and acting like a parachute to slow you down. Practise them and use them all the time.

Efficiency

In the sense of it being a skill, efficiency means doing everything you can to get the most out of yourself. Think of a car: driving efficiently means driving as far as you can per litre of fuel, so going easy on the accelerator, taking full advantage of downhills, always being in the right gear so not over-revving or labouring the engine. It's the same with cycling: you are trying to spread your effort, divide your energy by the distance. Riding efficiently helps you do this.

Tip_ Cadence

The most efficient cadence for cycling is around 90 revolutions per minute, a bit more on the flat and a little less going uphill. Next time you are riding on a flat, quiet road count your revolutions for 15 seconds and multiply by 4 to see where you are compared to this figure. You don't have to be spot on it, close will do. Monitor your pedalling frequently until you get a feel for 90rpm (some bike computers can measure revolutions, so the number is constantly displayed for you). Keep the 90rpm feel in mind whenever you are riding, especially during a sportive.

Perfect pedalling

The first rung on the efficiency ladder is making the most of each pedal revolution. As a skill that doesn't mean simply pushing harder, it means using a technique to deliver power from your legs to the pedals for as much of each pedal revolution as possible.

Four steps to perfect pedalling_

Step 01 Top dead centre

Mechanically in this phase it's difficult for you to apply power to your pedals, but it helps to drop your heel slightly to allow your legs to push the pedals forwards rather than down, thereby enabling you to push through dead centre, rather than push directly down against it.

Step 02 Power phase

This is the phase where you push down on the pedal, using your powerful thigh muscles to push the pedal towards the floor. However, progressively pointing your toes towards the floor through the second half of this phase brings your calf muscles into play to add to the power from the thigh muscles. Don't exaggerate the foot movement. A subtle flex of the foot is enough.

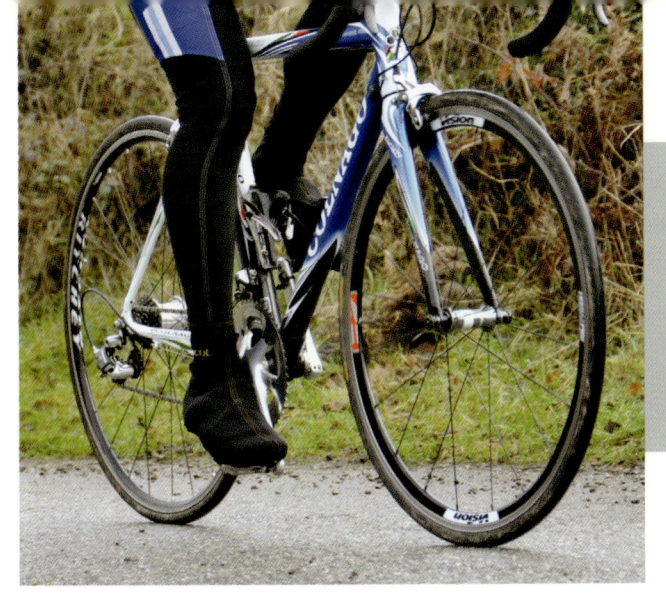

Step 03 Bottom dead centre

Just like top dead centre it's difficult to apply power here, but you can apply some if you claw your foot backwards. Imagine scraping something off the sole of your shoe on to the floor.

Step 04 Recovery phase

It used to be thought that the most efficient cyclists used their leg muscles to pull up on the pedals during this phase, but that's not true. What they do though is continue to point their toes, and this relaxes their thigh muscles and so prevents their ascending leg resisting the descending one when it's in its power phase.

003 : Cyclosportive Skills_

45

+ Drill: Perfect pedalling

This is best done with your bike on a turbo trainer, and you'll need a chair or stool. After a 10-minute warm-up of fast pedalling, detach one foot from the pedals and rest it on the chair. Pedal with the other leg in a low gear concentrating on turning the pedal as smoothly as possible. Your foot will instinctively flex as prescribed in the above steps. Pedal for 60 seconds, stop, swap the chair to the other side of your bike and do the same thing with your other leg. Repeat twice more for each leg.

> **Tip_ Visualisation**
> Don't think of pedalling as pushing down on your pedals, think of pushing them around. Pro bike racers call this action 'pedalling in circles'. And when someone is showing signs of being tired they call it 'pedalling in squares.'

Bike handling

The more you ride your bike the more you will become instinctively at one with it, and it will seem like an extension of your body. However, there are some skills you can learn that will help you around your first cyclosportive.

The most important is efficient cornering because it will help you take speed into and out of a corner, which saves effort, while at the same time staying upright, which saves skin. Safe and speedy cornering depends on taking the most efficient line through any given corner. However, overlying this are the prevailing traffic conditions around you. Out training there will be other road users to consider, and in an event there are other riders to compromise the best line.

This step-by-step guide demonstrates the best line though a right and left bend on British roads in ideal conditions, but always err on the side of caution.

Step 01

Assess the corner before you get to it – can you see all the way around it, how tight a corner is it? Adjust your speed according to what you have seen by braking while you are still travelling in a straight line.

Step 02

As you get closer to the bend check what is behind you by looking over your shoulder. There's a tendency to veer over to the side you are looking, so be aware of that and stay straight.

Step 03

For a left bend, check there is no traffic behind you, then move out slightly as this helps you take a straighter and therefore faster line through the corner. Shift to a lower gear as this will help you accelerate after the corner. For a right bend stay over on the far left of the road.

Step 04

Lean your bike into the corner. Keep your inside foot up and outside down. Move your weight over your outside leg, while pointing your inside knee into the corner. This subtle shift helps your bike turn. Aim your bike to cut across the apex of the bend, as this is the shortest route through it.

Step 05

Once out of the corner and when you are going straight, get out of the saddle to help accelerate quickly.

Essentially good cornering is about taking the racing line, which is the quickest way through a corner where you do not lose speed. Generally the racing line is an out (before the corner) in (going through the corner and cutting the apex) and out (where you end up on the road after the corner) sweeping movement.

Cornering is a skill worth practising. Taking the correct line through corners preserves speed, which means you don't have to make unnecessary efforts to gain it back with heavy acceleration after the corner. Add up the efforts of hard accelerations over a 160km event and they take their toll. Correct cornering saves energy and gives you a faster finishing time. Good cornering is speed for free.

Climbing

There are two ways to climb hills: in or out of the saddle. However, sportives are all about spreading your effort and riding efficiently, and the most efficient way to climb any hill is to sit in the saddle and pedal a low gear. It's not always the fastest way to climb, and it's not always possible, but more of that later. Climbing in the saddle is another golden rule to keep in mind.

+ Climbing in the saddle is energy efficient

Here's another mantra to bear in mind for sportives: balance power output at any given moment against that needed to last the whole distance.

It is also very important to keep your pace up over the top of a climb, until gravity begins to help on the descent. One of the worst things you can do in terms of economy of effort and lowering your average speed is to relax and slow once the climbing ends. It's understandable. You have made a big effort to get to the top of the climb, sometimes you feel like

Spreading the load_

Pedalling a low gear is often called spinning, which is a good word to visualise when you try to do it. Spinning a low gear is important because it saves your legs. Think about lifting weights. It's easier to lift 20kg in four lots of 5kg than all at once. That's what using a low gear uphill does; it effectively divides the amount you lift at one go (which is you and your bike) over more pedal revs. This causes less strain on your body because you do less work per movement, although the total amount moved is the same. Taking the weight analogy further, you wouldn't think twice about lifting a 5kg weight 10 times, but you instinctively know that lifting 50kg once exacts a larger physiological cost on your body, because you know it will make your muscles ache and make you breathe heavily. These are the sort of costs you need to drive down in sportives. It's the Tesco approach to cycling.

So, start thinking of hills you normally ride up like this. Shift to a lower gear at the beginning of each climb than you normally select, and sit and spin your way to the top. Once you get used to this you can think about gearing higher, but always spinning. You want to get up hills quickly, but not at the cost of leaving you exhausted at the top.

+ Standing up out of the saddle allows your upper body to help on steep climbs

congratulating yourself and enjoying your moment of conquest. Don't do it! All your work is wasted if you don't keep pushing until gravity really takes over. You simply aren't moving fast enough to back off at the top of a climb, so if you do back off you slow dramatically and it takes quite a while to build speed back up on the descent.

Your upper body plays a part when you climb too. You are going slower than on the flat so being aerodynamic isn't important. Sit more upright than you would on the flat with your hands on the top of your handlebars, or on the brake lever hoods, and angle your elbows out slightly. This gives your chest room to allow the deep, rhythmic breathing required on hills.

But what do you do when the hill gets really steep? You can use your arms and shoulders to help power you upwards, but sometimes it just becomes impossible to keep on riding in the saddle. You have shifted to your lowest gear but you are straining and not pedalling in nice smooth circles. To continue like this would unduly increase the physiological cost of riding. At that point climbing out of the saddle becomes a better option because you spread the load again – not only over more pedal revolutions this time but also over more muscles.

Smoothly lift yourself from the saddle and use your arms and shoulders to pull up on your handlebars as you push the pedals around. It's very important to keep applying pressure to the pedals during the transition from the saddle to standing. Many people don't – they pause – but doing that causes

Tip_ Visualisation
Pro bike racers have a saying, 'keep it lit', which means keep your effort up and keep pressure on the pedals as much as possible. Put those three words, 'keep it lit', in your mind and let them stay there. At the top of each climb think 'keep it lit'.

them to slow suddenly, which can result in any rider following closely behind to run into them.

Group riding

When cycling uphill the biggest force you fight is gravity. When cycling on the flat the biggest force you fight is air resistance, or drag as it's more correctly called. But where gravity remains constant, drag increases exponentially as you go faster. That's why efficient cycling on the flat means finding ways of cheating drag.

You can do it by sheltering in the slipstream of other riders, and when you can't you need to make your body as aerodynamic as possible. Sheltering in the slipstream of another rider saves you 60 per cent of the effort you would make to ride at the same speed on your own. And there is a skill to it, a skill so important that we'll keep coming back to it throughout the book.

First though let's look at making yourself as aerodynamic as possible for riding alone. To do this you need to think about occupying as little space as possible, and what controls the space you occupy is your height and width when you ride your bike. Lower your body into a crouch by bending your elbows to reduce your height, and keep your knees and elbows tucked in, or at least don't stick them out, to reduce your width. It doesn't sound much but being streamlined makes a huge difference to your energy consumption and your average speed over a sportive.

Think about this all the time you ride from now on. Think about getting your torso low and be aware

Pro tip_
'When I climb I try to visualise the best climbers that I've seen on the TV in the Tour de France. Just thinking about how they ride helps me ride faster and with an efficient fast cadence,' Richard Newey, top 10 finisher in the 4800km non-stop Race Across America.

+ Riding alone and staying low

of where your arms and legs are. You don't have to go to extremes – the rider in this picture is in a great position for riding fast on the flat. He's low, his elbows are tucked in and his forearms are level with the ground, so they are creating much less drag than if his arms were sticking straight down. A position like this might seem strange at first, but bear with it. To make riding like this easier you can do core strengthening exercises, which are demonstrated later in the book.

You can sit more upright and straighten your arms when you follow another rider because you are sheltering in his or her slipstream. It is also useful when climbing, because you are going slower and this crouched position isn't needed.

> **Tip_ Visualisation**
> Never look at the summit of the climb as the end of it. Instead visualise the summit as being 25–50m over the other side. This will help you to keep it lit over the top, which does wonders for your finishing time.

Cyclosportive_

Ride conservatively in your first cyclosportive. Follow other riders, get into a group where you feel comfortable with the pace and stay there. Avoid riding at the front of the group as much as possible, and the energy you save will pay dividends during the last stages of the ride. In the last quarter, if you feel good, then push on a bit. You can ride on your own then as you catch and pass riders in front of you.

As you progress though you'll find yourself in groups of riders nearer the front of the whole event. These groups will contain experienced men and woman who'll want you to share the pace with them. This is good cycling etiquette, so do it. Anyway, it means the group will be faster, which will do your finish time a lot of good.

To take your turn at pace setting you need to learn the skill of riding in a pace-line. This is quite simple if the wind is in front or behind the group. The rider at the front sets the pace and the rest follow in a line behind. When the front rider decides to stop setting the pace he or she moves out of the way and slows down. The next rider then takes up the pace setting, while the former pace setter slips down the line to join in the line again at the back. Simple!

The tricky bit comes when the wind is from the side. Then the line fans out on the road in the direction the wind is coming from. Have a look at this step-by-step explanation

Pro tip_
Following behind another rider saves energy, but exactly where you sit behind them – directly, a little to the left or to the right – depends on the direction of the wind. 'There's a place when you're behind another rider that gives you most shelter. To find it you have to move around a bit. Listen to the wind in your ears as you do, when the noise is least that's the place to be.' Team Sky pro, Russell Downing.

Step 01

In this sequence of pictures the wind is coming from the riders' left side. Here rider 1 is the furthest right in the picture, with the others inside and each one a little behind the other. This arrangement is called an echelon in cycle racing. The front and furthest right rider is taking the brunt of the side wind and the rest are effectively sheltering behind, so using much less energy.

Step 02

The front rider decides how far out in the road to ride. Once there are no spaces on his or her inside, the rest do not tag along in a line behind. If they did that they would all be riding in some of the wind. Instead they form another echelon behind the first one.

Step 03

When rider 1's turn at pace setting is done he eases his effort and slows down and drops back while moving towards the inside slightly. He or she does not ease off totally, keeps pedalling but with slightly less effort.

Cyclosportive_

Step 04

Rider 2 is now on the outside, so is setting the pace. At the same time rider 1 accelerates slightly to take the inside position in the echelon

Pro tip_
'When riding in an echelon it's important to ride as smoothly as possible, and never overdo anything. When your turn at pace setting is over, ease off slightly. When you move across the road, don't do it all at once, just drift back and towards the inside at an even, steady rate. Remember though, when you reach the end of a fast-moving echelon you need to accelerate sharply and quickly catch on to the end of it,' Barry Hoban, eight times a Tour de France stage winner.

Descending

Going downhill is the ultimate speed for free, so you have to make the descents on any course count. This doesn't mean throwing yourself downhill with total abandon; it means going down fast but in control.

To go fast you need to be low on your bike, and that also helps cornering at speed because it lowers your centre of gravity. Being low also involves holding the bottom of the handlebars, which at speed is the safest place to hold them as doing so distributes your weight around your bike as evenly as possible and makes you more stable.

Hold the bottom of your handlebars so that you can reach your brake levers easily, but don't ride with a finger or two touching the brake levers as some people do. You need all your fingers around your handlebars for safety. Hold firmly, but don't squeeze because that creates tension in your arms, shoulders and neck. If you hit a bump in the road any tension can cause you to go out of control and crash. Think of your arms as doing the job of shock absorbers on a car. They need to absorb bumps by bending at the elbow. But don't be too yielding, you must resist the bumps too, like dampening does in shock absorbers.

Lower your body so that it's parallel with the top tube of your bike, and sit towards the back of your saddle on straights. Keep your knees and elbows tucked in. Think of a downhill skier on a straight slope. That's what you are trying to emulate. Never copy the extreme off-the-saddle descending styles you will see some pros do in races such as the Tour de France. They are experts at bike control and practice this stuff for hours.

As you approach a corner you must start to reduce your speed. Still hold the bottom of your handlebars but sit up, so your upper body acts as an air-brake. Sticking your knees out helps with this too. Crouch before braking and apply your front then rear brake very slowly, and steadily increase your pull on the levers. Move your backside further back in the saddle as you do so, as this puts more weight over your rear wheel and will prevent skids.

Match your braking force to the steepness of the hill and tightness of each corner. Do the same with your body position. If you sit in a normal riding position going down a steep hill your weight isn't distributed the same as it is when you ride on the flat. Effectively there is more weight over the front wheel than the back, which is why you have to push your body back.

Once at a safe cornering speed just treat the corner like any other. The dynamics of cornering on a descent are similar to those on the flat. Try to use cambers to your advantage. This is where the road slopes upwards away from you. You can corner a bit quicker where there is a camber because it acts like the banking on a cycle racing track or velodrome. Avoid adverse cambers though, and if you can't then corner really slowly.

Try to look through the corner and pick your line according to the out–in–out principle of cornering. However, you must try to avoid loose gravel, mud and water on the road. If you can't then slow right down. You can usually see the line other vehicles take through corners on descents, and normally this is where you should follow on your bike.

Descending, particularly while negotiating corners, is a situation where experience counts. Good coaching counts too. If you know anyone who's an experienced rider, and in particular if they have taken part in road races, ask them if you can ride with them a few times. Follow their lines downhill and through corners and you'll soon pick up the skills of descending. Access to coaches is a good reason for joining a cycling club.

003 : Cyclosportive Skills

+ Hold the bottom of the handlebars on descents

Cyclosportive_

Eating and drinking

Drinking

Step 01

When riding on your own place one hand on the top of the handlebars, keep looking ahead and reach down for your bottle. However, if you are in a group or are going downhill it's best to keep your hand on the back brake lever hood so you can brake if necessary. You need to use the back brake because its effect is less severe. Front braking can make you unstable when riding one-handed. Therefore the hand you use to reach for your drink depends on whether you are a left- or right-hand back-braker.

Step 02

Still looking ahead, and without sitting up too much as this slows you down, raise the bottle to your lips, turn your head slightly, pull the bottle cap valve open with your teeth and drink. Squeezing the bottle helps this process.

Step 03

Again, keep looking forward at all times. Shut the bottle cap valve by pressing it against your chin then replace the bottle in its cage. You should practise this whole process until it is second nature. If you don't you will fumble this step and have to look down to help locate the bottle cage. This is one way that crashes happen in bunches.

Cyclosportive_

Eating

Step 01

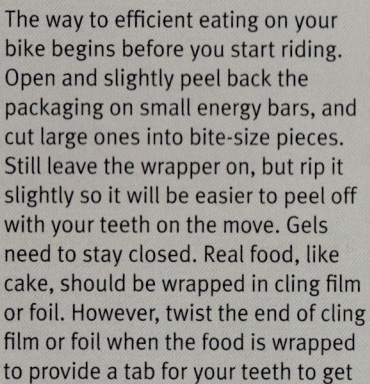

The way to efficient eating on your bike begins before you start riding. Open and slightly peel back the packaging on small energy bars, and cut large ones into bite-size pieces. Still leave the wrapper on, but rip it slightly so it will be easier to peel off with your teeth on the move. Gels need to stay closed. Real food, like cake, should be wrapped in cling film or foil. However, twist the end of cling film or foil when the food is wrapped to provide a tab for your teeth to get hold of when unwrapping.

Step 02

Always store food in the same pockets. Some racers prefer bars on one side and gels on the other. Some mix them up. Decide what works for you and stick to it, then you aren't fumbling around for what you need. It's best to store food in pockets so that it is balanced throughout the ride, so if you take one item from the left side pocket you take the next from the right.

Step 03

This is just like drinking. If you are alone, hold the top of the bars and reach into your pocket for the item of food you need. If you are riding in a group, cover the back brake. However, on long rides you might need to reach into all pockets, so you might need to cover the front brake and use your other hand. The key to avoiding problems here is knowing which item is in which pocket and being able to retrieve it quickly, which is why you should practise the correct technique a lot.

Step 04

Once you have what you want transfer it to your mouth, pull off the wrapper and eat the food. Always put the wrapper back in your pocket. Try to keep low while you eat, looking forwards all the time. Pick flat sections to eat on: eating downhill can be dangerous and eating uphill is near impossible.

The next step

Now you know what skills are required practise them until they become second nature. The next step is to prepare physically to meet the challenges of cyclosportives, so in the next chapter we outline what they are.

Case Study

Getting to grips with skills: Richard Bowley

Richard did a fair bit of cycling when he was younger, then had some time away from it doing other things. He took up cycling again a couple of years ago, having heard about the boom in cyclosportives from friends and reading about it in the cycling media.

He started training two years ago in response to a challenge one of his friends set himself to celebrate his fiftieth birthday. It was a tough one, a ride across the spine of the Pyrenees called the Raid Pyrenean, but the skills Bowley learned by doing it stood him in good stead for the cyclosportives he has subsequently done.

'Initially I thought the Raid Pyrenean would be a good boys weekend. I knew some proper cyclists were going, and by proper I mean some guys who raced or did sportives, plus there were others in the group who hadn't done much. Given that I thought I'd be able to mooch along in the middle somewhere.

I started training, and since I live in Cornwall, which has plenty of long hills, I thought I'd be OK on the climbs. I did a cyclosportive in Cornwall too as part of my preparation, but the big thing that caught me out in the Pyrenees wasn't the climbs – it was the descents.

Each of the stages we did were around 60 to 70 miles, with hardly any flat at all, so the Raid is a hell of a trek. On each stage we quickly got spread out, so you were in a little world of your own. The scenery was magnificent and cycling up Tour de France climbs like the Tourmalet was an inspiring experience.

Riding alone for hours on end gave me time to think about my cycling, and gave me the chance to experiment a bit. I quickly got the hang of spinning low gears up the climbs, but I also started to follow better riders down them too. I started taking the same lines as them into and out of bends, and I started getting faster because of it.

One descent really stands out. It was 35 kilometres long and had massive sweeping hairpins. I was on my own and decided to put everything I'd seen into practice. The feel of the flow of the bike as each straight went into a bend and out again was amazing – I think it was then that I learned to ride my bike properly. You can take minutes off your time just by going downhill and cornering faster.

I enjoyed my rides more at home after that trip, and I did more sportives. I lost a stone in weight too. Now, instead of being a bit intimidated by hills, I use them to gauge my fitness. If I'm able to sit on a climb where I used to have to ride out of the saddle, I know I'm getting fitter.

Since the Raid I've done some UK sportives, including the Exmoor Beast in terrible wind and rain when it was an achievement just to get to the end of it. I really enjoy cyclosportives, but as well as getting fit, I'd advise anyone to think about their bike skills and practice them as much as possible.'

003 : **Cyclosportive Skills**

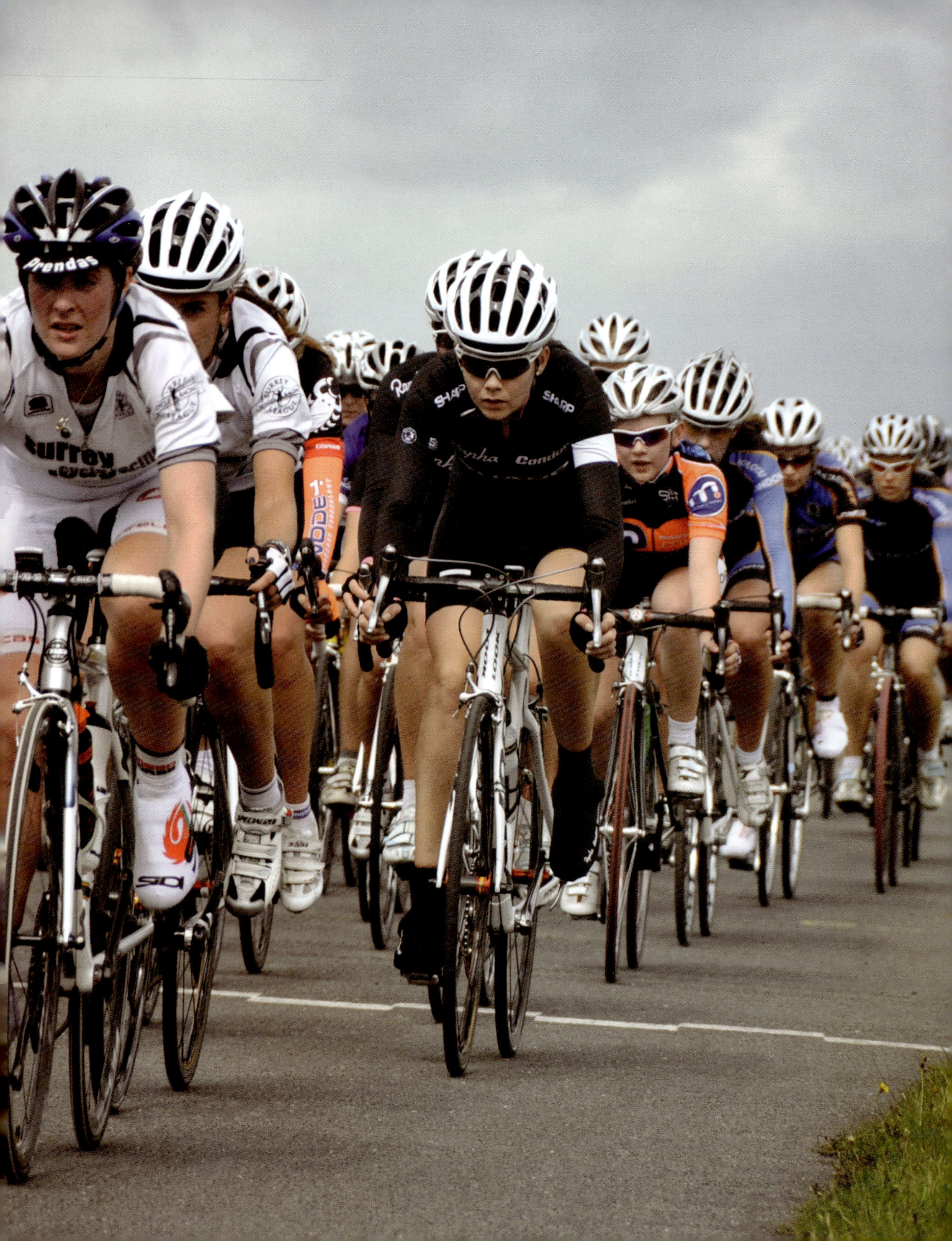
Prendas
SHARP
SHARP

+ Sportive Demands
[chapter : 004]

The demands of cyclosportives change slightly depending on your objectives, but they always combine elements of good physical fitness, sound equipment choice, optimal nutrition and the correct mental approach to training and the event. All are equally important and this cannot be stressed enough. Many people get hung up on the physical side of endurance events such as cyclosportives, but neglecting your bike, bad nutrition or not addressing the mental side of your training and approach to the event will limit and can undermine what you are capable of physically.

Fitness science

Basically fitness is the body's response to the demands placed on it. It is also quite a specific thing. A world-class marathon runner who doesn't cycle won't perform optimally (which would be up to their fitness level in the marathon) in a cycling event. Neither will a world-class cyclist who does no running perform in the marathon anywhere near the level they ride at. But even within a single activity, such as cycling, fitness has to be specific to the duration and intensity of that activity.

Cyclosportives are endurance events. A 50km sportive, about the shortest distance you'll find, will see you on your bike for around two hours. Maybe a bit less, but possibly more. Exercise theory says that endurance events are those where your aerobic system dominates energy supply. Aerobic means with oxygen. When you exercise aerobically your ability to deliver oxygen to your muscles, process it and thereby burn fuel to produce energy is the limiting factor.

Just to complicate things, some endurance events in cycling have a large anaerobic element. Anaeorobic means without oxygen, so in the human body that means energy production that doesn't require oxygen to burn fuel. This system gives instant power over and above the power you produce using oxygen to burn fuel, a bit like a car's turbo does. Anaerobic systems are important in endurance events lasting up to five minutes, but play a dwindling role after that.

Sports scientists define endurance events as anything where the aerobic system dominates, which is anything over about 90 seconds, so cyclosportives are definitely endurance events. Anaerobic energy production has little bearing on how you perform in cyclosportives, except if you are going for a super-fast time and want to contend for a top place in your age group. But more of that

> **Pro tip_**
> 'We are so sure that riding long distances puts something extra, some sort of in-depth strength, into your legs that we even have sprinters like Sir Chris Hoy put in a two-week, high-mileage block of training close to races that they are peaking for,' Shane Sutton, Head Coach of British Cycling.

later. However, some anaerobic training improves your cycling efficiency and pushes up the pace you can ride at for extended periods of time, which are both very important in cyclosportives.

Endurance 101

Cyclosportives are long-distance cycling challenges – they are endurance events with bells on. And if your event is long distance then it figures that some of your training should be done over long distances. Not every ride needs to be a long one. Indeed your emphasis in terms of the number of training sessions you do should be on short ones, because they develop crucial aspects of your fitness that make you ride better over long distances. Short-distance sessions can improve your average speed over a long ride. Some short sessions can even trick your body into thinking it's ridden a long distance.

However, one undeniable fact remains: your performance in a 50km sportive is determined by, among other things, getting a few two-hour rides in your legs. And the experience of a 160km sportive will be a much happier one if you have ridden for four hours on at least a couple of occasions.

The fat–glucose fuel swing

When you exercise lightly you burn fat as fuel. As the intensity of exercise increases you begin to burn glucose, which is stored in your muscles and liver as glycogen, as well as fat. As exercise intensity increases, the proportion of glucose to fat burned increases. Continue to go harder and glucose burning exceeds fat burning and continues to do so as intensity increases until, when you are pushing at your aerobic limit, almost all your energy is provided by glucose.

It's an elegant system that has one flaw. Where even the skinniest person has enough fat reserves

> **Cycling fact_**
> (Well, all endurance sports actually...) Trainers of racing cyclists and of marathon runners have always intuitively understood that their athletes need to ride and run long distances to reach their potential, as well as doing a lot of other kinds of training, although they were never sure why. For many years training theory held that if you broke distances into chunks, and rode and ran those chunks faster than the pace you wanted for the full event distance, this should be the best preparation for the event distance. Sports science, as it was understood, firmly believed that you didn't need to train over the distance or duration of the event. The thing is though, those who did train over the full duration of their events often performed better than those who didn't.

> **Important discovery_**
>
> Because they are open-minded individuals, sports scientists kept investigating this 'long-distance works' anomaly, and recently they made an important discovery. Long rides (long runs too – but this is a cycling book) trigger the production of an immune system compound called interleukin-6 (IL-6), which triggers increased fat burning to produce energy. And the thing that starts the production of IL-6 is glycogen depletion – glycogen being the substance that carbohydrates are stored by the body as. A chemical reaction splits glycogen into glucose, which is burned in the muscles to produce energy as it's needed. The thing is though, you can't dawdle on these long rides. You have to ride quite hard too.

004 : **Sportive Demands**_

to keep them going all day, most of us only have about two hours of glucose to burn. By eating and drinking while you exercise you can take on carbohydrates, which break down into glycogen to be stored in the body, then glucose when needed in the muscles. But this energy supply is still finite when you are pushing really hard. It's what coaches call a limiter.

The solution would be for your body could increase the threshold of exercise intensity it could support by burning fat. That would spare your glycogen stores, which would be used at a much slower rate. That is what long rides do. Long rides trigger IL-6 production, which increases the capacity of an athlete to burn fat to produce energy. This spares your glycogen stores. You just become a more efficient, lean-burning engine.

Going long

There are two ways to stimulate the production of IL-6; doing occasional long rides, or increasing the total volume of training you do. However, for someone training for cyclosportives, long rides also bring about a number of other event-specific changes, which makes them doubly important.

The other good thing is you don't need many of these long rides to switch on the IL-6 response, but as we said before they need to be quite hard. Sportive events will switch on the response too. So a few long rides, and regular events throughout the year will keep you ticking over in lean-burn engine mode.

Long rides also increase the efficiency of your pedalling, which in itself means you will use less total energy at a given speed. They also train specific support muscles, in your neck and hands for example, that nothing else does quite as well.

They have positive effects on many other physical aspects of your cycling too, but they are essential in developing the mental approach that helps you succeed in cyclosportive. Long rides give you the

+ Specific muscles in the neck and hands need to be trained too

> **Cycling fact_**
> Coping with riding a long distance is the number one demand of cyclosportives.

confidence that you will complete the distance on event day, and they increase your comfort threshold. This is very important. Very often the ability to tough it out on the day is one of the key success factors in a sportive. Long rides get your body accustomed to the discomfort of hours in the saddle; you get used to how it feels and after a while you don't notice niggling discomforts like you used to.

Upping the cruise

Upping your average speed is another key demand of a cyclosportive. To get a good time you need to ride fast, but don't think that going fast is just what you do on straight bits or on the climbs of the course. It means going as fast as you can over the whole course.

And that in itself breaks down into two further concepts: spreading your effort over the whole distance; and preserving speed through corners, on descents and over the tops of hills. We can't emphasis enough about correct pacing in cyclosportives. Practise spreading your effort evenly on some of your training rides. Practise

eating and drinking too, until you have perfected a nutritional strategy that supports your efforts.

Preserving speed through corners, using hills correctly, is all part of the big cyclosportive mantra – speed for free. We talk about cornering, climbing and descending in chapter 3 (Cyclosportives Skills), but they have a big effect on your average speed.

Tackle the terrain

Hills have been regarded as the testing ground of cycling almost since the sport of cycle racing began. It's no coincidence then that there are very few flat sportives. If enduring the distance is the first cyclosportive demand, mastering hills is a close second.

Don't let this put you off. No matter who you are you can become a better climber. You'll even come to embrace hills and mountains, and the enormous satisfaction of conquering them.

The demand of hills is partly met through skill, which we've already covered, and partly through training, which we cover in chapter 5 (Sportive

Training). Training also includes the right mental approach to climbing hills in a cyclosportive. The key here is never to be daunted by the length of steepness of a climb. Concentrate instead on what you are doing on each section of it. Focus on the here and now, on doing the section you are on perfectly.

Don't be downhearted either if you live in a totally flat area. Hills can be simulated when riding a flat road into the wind, and they can be simulated on a turbo trainer. Also one small climb can become a mountain if you ride up it enough times.

Lucien Van Impe comes from the Belgian region of Flanders, a place with no mountains at all. When he trained he would ride to his nearest short, sharp hill and go up it as many as 10 times, sometimes in the saddle, sometimes out, sometimes revving a small gear and sometimes pushing a larger one to build strength. You just need to be adaptable.

The weather

This is a less predictable demand, but a very important one. In southern Europe it can be extremely hot, and the wind and rain can be treacherous. Mix mountains into that and weather

> **Pro tip_**
> 'Start every climb in a lower gear than you need for the whole climb. Concentrate on controlling your breathing first too. Then when you are in control, that's when to accelerate. Shift to the gear you need for the climb and start to apply the pressure, and accelerate towards the top.' Lucien Van Impe, 1976 Tour de France winner and six times king of the mountains

has the potential to stop events taking place. Strangely enough, in northern Europe the seasons are more predictable so the weather is less of a factor in cyclosportives.

The big weather factors are heat and humidity, rain and cold. Each needs to be dealt with through a combination of correct clothes, nutrition and pre-event adaptation. With the help of this book, and as your cycling experience grows, you'll work out what works for you. But remember to try new things in training, not in an event

Getting your clothing wrong can be the difference between success and failure in a cyclosportive event, so follow the guidelines in Getting Started, including the tips about preparing for extreme heat and cold (*see* page xxx).

Nutrition is dealt with in its own chapter – chapter 6 – and pre-event adaptation is mostly to do with improving your fitness, but there is one thing worth taking on board now. It's to do with something mentioned throughout the book, upping your comfort zone.

Without overdoing it, it's worth doing some training rides in the rain and cold. The same goes for training in hot conditions. It might be easier to replace an outdoor training session when

Case history_

One of the key things in bad weather is not to let it get you down, just focus on what you are doing and you will get through. Take this example of the experience of a 70-year-old, Ron Keegan, who took part in and finished the 2009 Exmoor Beast sportive, which was held at the beginning of November in gale-force winds and heavy rain.

'Nearly 2000 entered but 600 decided that discretion was the better part of valour, thinking at least they'd live to fight another day. Amazingly though, of the thousand or so who did start most battled through. It was as if we all made some sort of grizzly pact not to give in and let the day beat us.

'I rode a hybrid bike, which turned out just right for the job, and as I was riding with my daughter, Janine, we planned to take it steady and get through come what may. I felt in control in the wind, and the low gears meant I kept riding where others walked. I'll never forget going up Dunkery Beacon. Out of the mist a woman was standing beside the cattle grid, dressed in a trench coat and riding hat, saying in a posh voice, 'Do be careful, it's like a skating rink,' to every rider who passed. It was one of those days for seeing things like that.

'The organisers should have run two events, a 160km and 100km, but they wisely decided to put all their resources behind the 100km. Dunkery was a pivotal point of the ride. Despite the conditions some still wanted to do the 160km, but Dunkery put them straight. Wheels were spinning on the slick surface, riders just got off mid-pedal, causing those behind to do the same. And all the time a 80km/h headwind lashed stinging rain into our faces. Nobody wanted to do the 160km after Dunkery, and it took some as much as four hours to complete the first 55km.

Things improved at Simonsbath, where the organisers set up wood-burning stoves and served hot soup to everyone who got there. That was a nice prelude to the best bit, as the wind now blew behind us and 40km/h was easy on the road to Wheddon Cross.

Finally we reached the last descent and the indoor finish at the Butlins holiday camp in Minehead, where everyone clutched their 'I Tamed the Beast' kit bag, sipped champagne and shared their memories.'

---

the weather is less than perfect with an indoor one, and often that is a good idea. Training outdoors in cold, wet or very hot conditions places extra strain on your body. Nor will you be able to train optimally. The thing is though, occasional rides done in these conditions will up your comfort zone, enabling you to push on through the weather if it is less than ideal for the event.

Mental challenge

Pushing through adverse conditions brings us to the mental challenge of cyclosportives. There is a state of mind for these long-distance events that you need to cultivate. It's a mixture of patience and concentration, with a sprinkling of toughing it out.

Patience involves not starting too fast, never getting involved in battles other than your own with the event, and not overdoing it on any single part of the route. Bear this in mind on the day of the event. You've trained very hard, probably looked forward to what you are about to do for months. Imagined all the different scenarios. You will be in a heightened state of awareness on the start line, simply raring to go. The danger now is that you'll start too fast.

To avoid doing that monitor how you are breathing, or maybe use a heart-rate monitor all the time in the event. You know what your heart rate is normally in training. If, for example, you are seeing numbers at the start of a 160km event that you normally see while doing a 20-minute hard interval, you have to back off. It's the same for your breathing. You know how hard you breathe for given efforts. Don't listen to your legs, the sensations in them aren't reliable because adrenalin interferes with the effort/discomfort link in muscles.

On the other hand there might be someone you want to beat, which is fine. Healthy rivalry is what drives sport. However, if you are pushing too hard – breathing heavily or seeing higher heart-rate numbers than you know you'll be able to sustain for the distance – let it go. Your rival may well be pushing too hard and you'll catch up later, when he or she will probably be shattered.

Focus on the whole

Some parts of the route can occupy a bigger place in your mind than the rest. This is especially true of events in the great mountain ranges, which may include one or more of the most famous climbs used in the Tour de France, or the Tours of Italy or Spain. It's exciting to ride these climbs, but it's also easy to get carried away. You are eager to get to the top, to have bagged one of the giants, but the effort you make must be set in context with the rest of the route. If it's the final climb then go hard, remembering of course the golden rule of starting the climb within yourself and building your effort towards the summit. If it is early in the route then remember it is no more important than any other section, and dose your effort accordingly.

The best way to describe the state of mind required for sportives is to think of living in the moment, but at the same time dividing the moments by the whole route. What that means is spreading your effort over the whole, but performing the pacing calculations necessary to do that is the only time you should think of the event as a whole.

The rest of the event should be viewed in terms of what you are doing now. Split it down into a series of monitoring questions about where you are now.

+ Are you going too fast or too slow for the section you are on?
+ Are you eating and drinking according to your overall plan?
+ Are you aerodynamic?
+ Are you pushing the pedals around or pedalling them around in circles?
+ Monitor everything, do not let anything slip and live in the here and now. Above all, while you have to be aware of how far there is to go in the event, never let that thought dominate.

Lastly we come to what can be the biggest challenge of cyclosportives, toughing it out. This is not an easy thing you've chosen to do, and it's best to accept that. After all, their toughness are what makes cyclosportives such a worthwhile challenge. Some of the top events are very hard. Most people who have done both say that the Etape du Tour, to take just one example, is much harder than running a marathon. And there are many events similar to the Etape. You might be on your bike for a very long time. It might be extremely hot, or cold and wet. You could feel quite isolated at times, scared even. Hopefully this book will help you overcome such situations, but in the end it will be down to you.

When things look bad, hang tough and muscle your way though. You will feel justifiably proud when you do. But to do that you need to prepare properly, so the next chapter looks at how to train for cyclosportives in general and how to prepare for your first ones in particular.

> ### Exception_
>
> We talk about this in chapter 7 (Going further), but it's still worth saying now. If you are after a fast time or a high placing, there are times when it pays to push a little bit harder so you can get with a fast group. However, you need experience, plus great fitness, to get this right, so leave it until later.

004 : **Sportive Demands**

Case Study

A veteran of the Race Across America talks about going the distance: Richard Newey

The Race Across America (the RAAM) is a big challenge – 3005 miles, over 100,000 feet of climbing. Solo competitors take between nine and twelve days to complete it, riding 350-500 miles per day, every day. It is longer than the Tour de France, but there are no stages and no rest days. When the flag drops in Oceanside, by the Pacific, the clock starts, and it only stops when each competitor reaches Annapolis on the Atlantic coast. Sleep happens when it has to.

Cyclosportives are a long-distance cycling challenge too, so we asked someone who has experienced the RAAM to talk about how he prepared for and met its demands. The British long-distance racer Richard Newey finished eighth in his first solo attempt in 2009, and plans to go back to the RAAM one day and do even better. He talks about how he trained for the RAAM, and how he dealt with the challenge of its enormous distance.

'I broke it down; just like I broke down my long rides in my training. I had a specific objective for each ride I did in training and was careful to achieve it. I did that by trying to always be in the moment and not looking too far ahead.

I tried not to think of the race very much when I trained, or even about my whole programme – I had worked that and my race strategy out with my coach and support team. The important thing to do in any training session is to commit to it and really focus on it. If you do each session to the best of your ability your plan will work.

People are surprised that I did a lot of training off my bike. You cannot simulate riding the RAAM. It involves riding 3000-odd miles by breaking them down into lots of 300 and slipping a couple of hours of sleep in between each one. That means you cannot bring about in training some physical adaptations you need, especially in small muscles that are crucial in the RAAM, but are hard to train just by cycling. To strengthen those muscles I did conditioning exercises like Bikram Yoga.

My strategy in the race was to break it down into sections and only concentrate on that section. If you ride for 1500 miles and think, "Oh my God, I've got another 1500 to ride" you'll never get there. I broke the whole thing into 300-mile sections, and would only think of the next after each one was complete.

The RAAM is incredibly mentally taxing. There were some dark moments where I experienced overwhelming tiredness and even hallucinations. Self-belief helps you get through these, but often for me the crucial help was thinking about all the people who supported me. It's a good idea to get a support group around you when you are doing anything like a sportive. Get them to invest in what you are doing. They really help you battle through during the difficult days.

My overwhelming advice is live in the moment, both in training and the race. Then you need to believe you can achieve what you are doing.

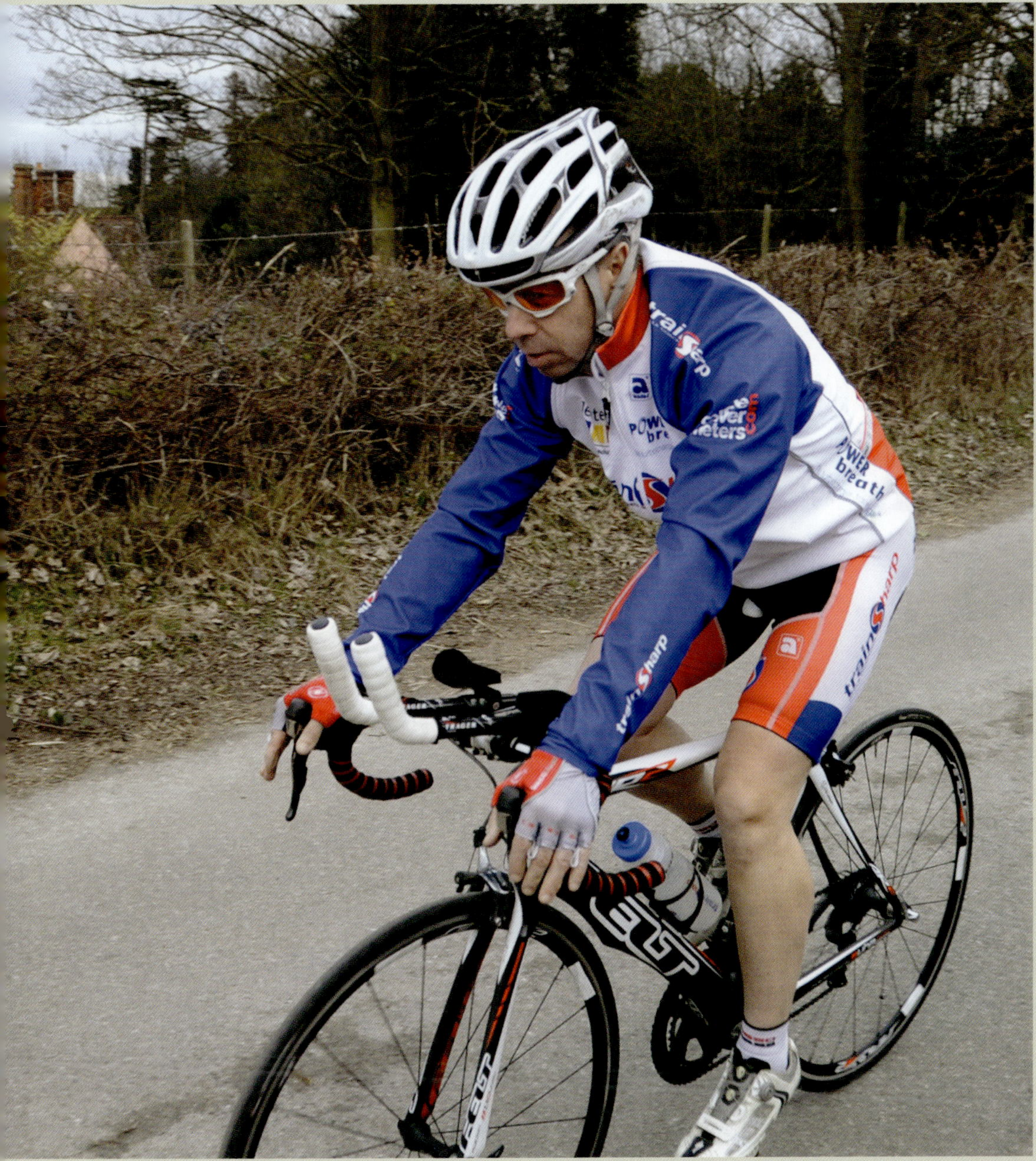
trainSharp
POWER breathe

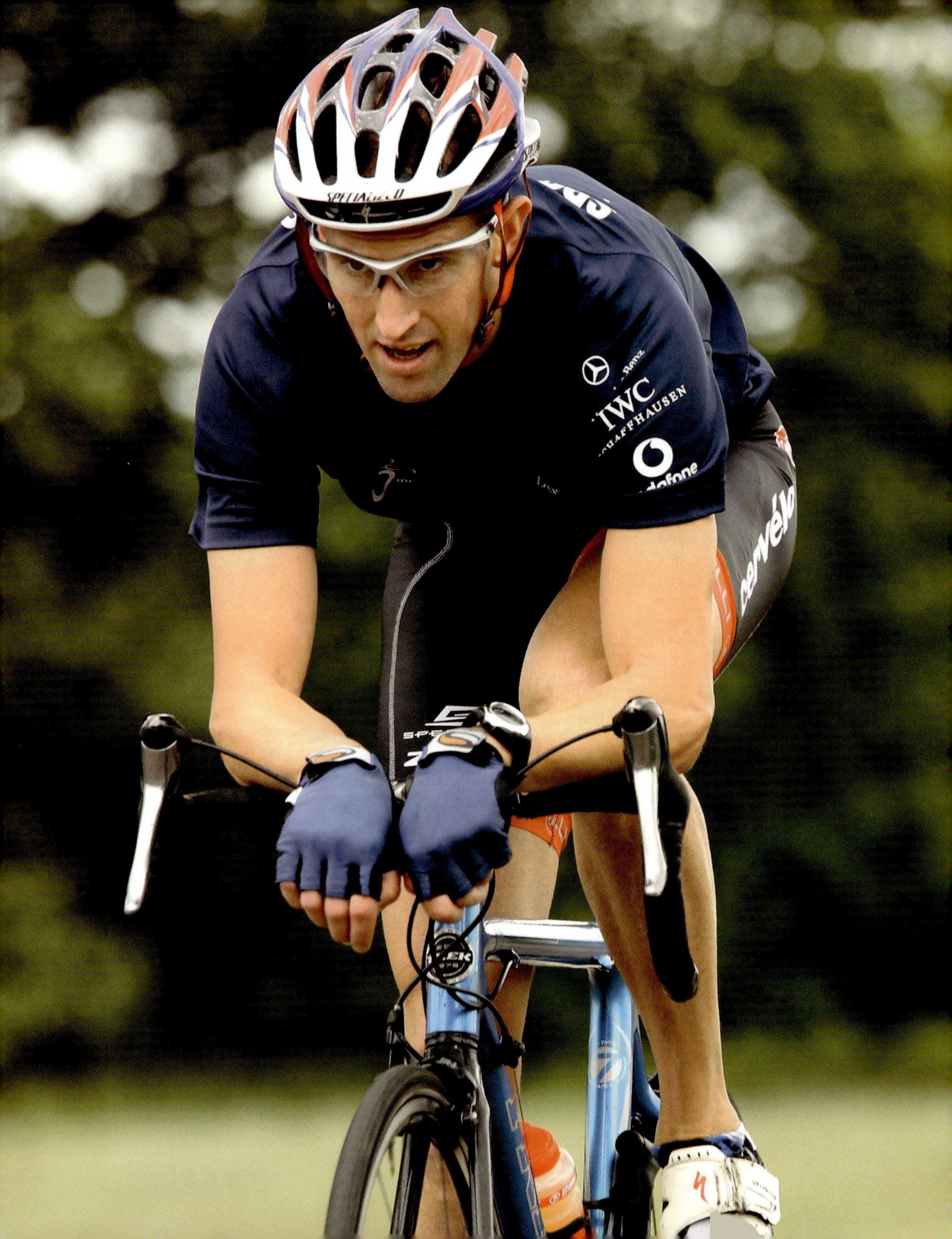
IWC

+ Sportive Training
[chapter : 005]

Although cyclosportives are long-distance endurance events, training for them isn't just a matter of riding long distances all the time, although a limited amount of long rides has its place. The most efficient way to train is to improve certain key capacities your body has to power a bike. And although these capacities might look as though they have little to do with riding a bike a long way, they are crucial and back each other up, to make you a better cyclist and well able to cope with the specific challenges of cyclosportives.

Key capacities

This is the maximum pace you can ride at for the following durations:

+ Ten to twenty seconds
+ Three to five minutes
+ One hour
+ Two hours

Not all of the above are as important as each other. You don't need telling that your speed when riding for one hour is far more important than the speed you can ride at for 20 seconds. However, the latter does have a bearing on the former, as have all the other durations on each other.

The pace you can ride at for these durations is crucial because your body is using different physiological systems to produce the power necessary to do it, and these systems all require training because they have a positive role in making you a better cyclist. We'll start looking at them from the shortest time upwards to appreciate better how they fit together.

Ten to twenty seconds

This represents the maximum power your body can produce going absolutely flat out, and as such probably looks as far removed from the demands of a 160km sportive as you can get, but it isn't. By increasing the absolute power you can transmit to the pedals, you increase the efficiency of your cycling. In short this means you can put in more power for less fuel, a significant factor in long-distance riding. Also, done in a certain way, very short intervals are good at building core strength. You don't need much training at this intensity, but it is still very important.

Three to five minutes

Riding as hard as you can at a constant pace for three to five minutes, where at the end of that period you can hardly ride any further, is a measure of something called your VO_2 max. It's the maximum amount of oxygen your body can process while exercising, and is a limiter on performance in endurance sports. Every individual has a pre-set genetic limit to the maximum amount of oxygen they can process while exercising, but up to that limit it is very trainable.

Again, like the 10- to 20-second intensity, you don't have to train very often at your VO_2 max (except if you decide to become very competitive once your experience builds, when you should do a little more). However, training that pushes your VO_2 max towards its potential will increase your endurance and your pedalling efficiency. It also has a bearing on the pace you can ride at for one hour, and the overall average pace you ride at in a sportive.

One hour

Years ago exercise scientists discovered that there was an optimal pace cyclists can ride at where their bodies just about keep up with processing the fuel they need and removing the by-products of exercise. You can keep up this pace for about one hour before other factors come into play that tend to slow you down. But go any harder within that hour and you have to slow down to recover.

This pace has been given all sorts of fancy names, such as anaerobic threshold. But referring to it as a threshold can be misleading as it's more a zone of transition. So we'll call it 'one-hour power'. You will dip in and out of this intensity a lot in cyclosportives, and improving your one-hour power has a direct bearing on your average speed. One-hour power is very trainable, and training it will also help increase your VO_2 max and efficiency at the same time.

Two hours

A lot of very important changes occur in your body when you exercise at the intensity you can keep up for two hours. These changes are crucial when training for cyclosportives, not only because this is the intensity you will ride at for much of the event, but also because the changes have a direct effect on increasing your physical endurance and efficiency in a sportive-specific way. These rides, which we refer to as level 2 rides (*see* p.xxx), will play a big part in your training and are a big part of your event.

The recipe

Although these durations are crucial, they don't mean that you have to stick to them exactly in training. They are simply the physical capacities you need to train to take part in and improve at cyclosportives. They are the ingredients of a cake if you like, and you chop them up into smaller units of time, adding them to the mix in different proportions.

For example, riding for one minute at your three-to-five-minute pace will improve it. And you can improve your one-hour power by exercising for periods of 20 minutes a few notches under it, and for four to five minutes a few notches over it, for example. These periods of exercise are called intervals, and interval training will form a crucial part of your regime.

But how do you know when you are exercising at these different capacities? You need a measure, and the one most often used in endurance exercise today is exercise intensity expressed in terms of levels or zones.

Different authorities suggest differing numbers of levels or zones, but to keep things simple we've chosen five. You also need something to provide feedback as to whether you are exercising at the prescribed level. You can assess this by how it feels, or use a measure such as a heart-rate monitor, because the levels can be expressed in terms of a percentage of maximum heart rate. To ascertain your maximum heart rate you can either subtract your age from 220, which for a 50 year old gives a maximum heart rate of 170 beats per minute. Or you can perform a maximum heart-rate test.

You can make the determination and zoning of training intensity levels very complicated and very precise, and that degree of application is required for many aspects of cycling. However, the primary challenge of cyclosportives is riding long distances, so it doesn't pay to get bogged down in the minutiae of intensity levels. The changes you need to bring about in your body are quite straightforward.

There is one tweak worth noting, though, one little sub-division of the training level table, which applies to level 2 and 3 and is very important in training for sportives. There is a small window of transition between upper level 2 and lower level 3 that, if you train in it, gives big returns for time invested. It's so effective that some people call

Maximum heart-rate test_

You need to be well rested to do this. Design a 5km route that ideally ends on the top of a hill. Put on your heart-rate monitor and warm up by riding for at least 20 minutes, pushing progressively harder all the time. Then do three 15-second flat-out sprints, with two minutes of easy pedalling in a low gear between each one. This warm-up should take you to the start of your 5km route. Start the route, riding at a pace that's as hard as you can just keep up for the whole 5km. Continue this effort on the hill, then for the last 200m of it go as fast as you can. Your maximum heart rate is the figure you see at the top of the hill.

+ The five exercise intensity levels

Level	Perceived effort	Percentage of maximum heart rate
1	Easy, just turning the pedals over, can speak easily	←---65%
2	From being able to speak freely but still feeling like you are making a sound effort, to only being able to speak in sentences before catching a breath. A good solid riding pace	66–80%
3	Difficult to speak, the pace you could keep up for 20–30 min and, at a push, for 1 hr, but only just	81–90%
4	Can't speak at all, the pace you could keep up for 3–5 min before slowing	91% plus
5	Flat out for 20 sec	Not applicable

> **Cycling fact_**
> The total volume of training is the factor that gives you the biggest fitness gains when preparing for cyclosportive events, so long as you recover between sessions. And to refine that the best results come if you spread the volume of training you do over more days per week.

it the 'sweet spot' of training, but we'll refer to it as 'upper tempo' because that gives more of a feel for the pace involved. It's a pace you have to concentrate on to maintain, but it doesn't feel an all-out effort like full-on level 3 does. Riding at this level is important because it pushes up the pace you can ride at level 3, or your one-hour power, from below, but does so while not being as demanding as riding at level 3. You recover quicker and can do more total work riding at upper tempo than at level 3.

Training diary

This is crucial. You can do it any way you want, but somewhere and somehow you must keep a record of all the training you do. Record your weight each day or so, record how much sleep you have had each day, your waking pulse rate and how you feel. In particular note down any illnesses you get.

Your diary will present a picture of how you react to training. For example, if you have a good event or feel particularly strong in a training session, look back at the training you did over the previous three weeks and that will be a good mix of sessions for you.

Recording your waking pulse shows how well you recover from training. If it is normally 60 and a reading of 65 pops up one morning, it means you either haven't recovered from the training you've done or you might be fighting off a cold or an infection. Whatever, it's the sign either to miss that day's training or to have an easy day.

Your diary will also show how you react to new training sessions, and to increasing the duration or intensity of your training. Over the years it will become your personal training manual, showing what training does and doesn't work for you.

First-timer's training plan

To do your first cyclosportive, say an 80km event, you now know enough theory to begin training. All you need is a training plan to act as a map to help you get there.

Plans are good. Especially if you don't have any experience of training. They tell you what to do on certain days of each week, but they don't suit everyone's circumstances. So, although the plans in this book can act as a guide, giving you the feel for the doses of training you need to include during each week, try to draw up your own plans once you gain some experience. This is especially true if your work patterns don't fit a five-days-a-week-weekends-off pattern.

Use your training diary to work out which training suits you. Add in what weaknesses and strengths you discovered in your first sportives. Use training sessions to target weaknesses and strengths. After all, you know where or in what part of your cyclosportive events you have struggled, so you need to tailor your training to address those problems.

Varied terrain

You also need a variety of roads to use with your training plan. Flat roads, hilly and rolling roads should feature in your training so you are ready for any terrain. If you don't have all these where you live, be creative. For example, you can simulate a rolling road on a flat one by alternating from a gear ratio that gives your normal pedalling rate to a higher one where you are labouring a bit.

If you live in a hilly area you could re-use the same piece of flat road for a flat session, or do flat rides on a turbo trainer. I live in a very hilly area, so I use an old railway line that has been converted to cycle use for my flat rides.

Conversely if it's dead flat where you live and your turbo trainer has a resistance mechanism, you can

Hill repeats_

You'll need to know how to do this training session for the 80km sportive plan.

+ Pick a steep hill that takes 1–2 minutes to climb.
+ Warm up for 15–20 minutes.
+ Ride up the hill as hard as you can, ensuring that you continue your effort over the summit.
+ Freewheel down the hill, the same side as you've just climbed or the other.
+ Repeat the climb 4 times to start with then add one extra climb each time you do the session, to a maximum of 10 climbs.
+ After that focus on increasing the speed at which you climb the hill by recording your times. Go for beating your fastest time, and your fastest average for the session. This ensures progressive improvement.

+ Practising with a mountain bike can be beneficial

simulate hills on that. Just turn up the resistance and raise the front of your bike up on a block of wood to simulate riding uphill. Riding off road on a mountain bike is another way of simulating hills, because the loose surfaces are harder to pedal on or because there are often short, sharp hills and banks in woods and on heathland. Always be adaptable and imaginative with your training.

Level 2

Level 2 riding is a crucial part of training for cyclosportives, especially when you start out. At this level you increase the size of your heart and the efficiency with which it delivers blood, and with it oxygen and fuel, to your muscles. Level 2 also increases the efficiency of chemical reactions that take place within your muscles. This level represents a large bandwidth of effort: 66–81 per cent of your maximum heart rate, or from being able to speak freely to having to concentrate on your breathing if you go on feel. When you do level 2 rides try to push up and down through the whole of this intensity range.

Understanding the training plan

The training plans we've drawn up are all 12 weeks long, which is a good length of time for targeting a single event. You will find it easier to focus on training for a specific event over this length of time, while it is enough to allow significant gains in fitness. So choose an event you want to take part in then count back 12 weeks and begin the plan. Use a similar training period when planning future events, and as you become more experienced you can use other cyclosportives within each 12-week training period as key training sessions.

The plan builds in three phases of three weeks, each phase a little more demanding than the last. Each week is also slightly harder than the one before. Every fourth week between the phases is an easier week to ensure recovery and it allows your body to adapt to the progressive demands you've placed on it. This three-weeks-hard, one-easy-cycle of training is the best way to ensure your fitness progresses, which it does by being pushed along with slightly harder sessions, then being allowed some recovery to make adaptations.

The table on page 78 isn't a training plan for beginners. You need to do some general riding before starting this plan and be able to complete three sessions of one hour at a good pace, plus a slower one of two hours in a week.

First long event

While 80km events are a good place to start, most cyclosportives are 100km or over, and the true classics are 160km or more. To prepare for a longer sportive you could just take the 80km plan and double it, but that isn't the most time efficient way, neither will it help you achieve your full potential.

Training for a 160km sportive requires a little bending of the fitness curve that simply riding more kilometres won't achieve. It involves training more precisely, and in a way that you get more for less. To do that there are a few short-cut training sessions that you should include. One of them is a way of tricking your body into thinking it's trained for longer, and therefore adapting accordingly. The other works on your VO_2 max.

On-off switches

This can really only be done on a turbo trainer, but it is very effective at improving your efficiency and core strength. Two things that are crucial in long-distance cycling. Efficiency means you go faster,

> **Cycling fact_**
> To improve any aspect of your fitness your training must push that aspect a little harder than your body is used to. This initiates a specific genetic response that tells your body to become stronger in that aspect. But remember, the training is just the stimulus. The response and strengthening only occur when you rest, and if you supply your body with the right nutritional building blocks for it to use.

Cyclosportive

+ Training plan for an 80km cyclosportive

	Monday	Tuesday	Wednesday	Thursday	Friday	Saturday	Sunday
Week 1	Ride @ level 2 for 60 min on a flat route	Rest	Ride @ level 2 for 60 min on a rolling route, upper level 2 (upper tempo) uphill	Rest	Ride @ level 2 for 75 min on a flat route (mid-way 15 min @ upper tempo)	Rest	Ride @ levels 1 and 2 for 90 min on a flat route
Week 2	Rest	Ride @ level 2 for 60 min on a rolling route, upper tempo uphill	Rest	Ride @ level 2 for 60 min on a flat route (middle 20 min @ upper tempo)	Rest	Ride @ level 2 for 40 min on a flat route (3 × 15-sec sprints mid-way with 5 min @ levels 1 and 2 between	Ride @ levels 1 and 2 for 100 min on a flat route
Week 3	Rest	Ride @ level 2 for 70 min on a rolling route, upper-tempo uphill	Rest	Ride @ level 2 for 60 min on a flat route (mid-way ride 2 × 10 min @ upper tempo with 5 min @ level 1 between)	Rest	Ride @ level 2 for 60 min on a flat route	Ride @ levels 1 and 2 for 120 min on a flat route
Week 4	Ride @ level 2 for 40 min on a flat route	Rest	Ride @ level 2 for 60 min on a flat route	Rest	Ride @ level 2 for 60 min on a flat route	Rest	Ride @ levels 1 and 2 for 90 min on a flat route
Week 5	Ride @ level 2 for 60 min on a flat route	Rest	Ride @ level 2 for 75 min on a rolling route, upper tempo, level 3 uphill	Rest	Ride @ level 2 for 60 min on a hilly route, upper tempo uphill	Rest	Ride @ levels 1 and 2 for 120 min on a rolling route.
Week 6	Rest	Ride a hill-repeats session	Ride @ level 2 for 60 min on a flat route	Ride @ levels 1 and 2 for 75 min on a rolling route	Rest	Ride @ level 2 for 60 min on a flat route	Ride @ levels 1 and 2 for 140 min on a rolling route

	Monday	Tuesday	Wednesday	Thursday	Friday	Saturday	Sunday
Week 7	Rest	Ride @ level 2 for 60 min (mid-way ride 15 min @ level 3)	Ride @ level 2 for 60 min	Ride @ level 2 for 60 min on a hilly route (mid-way ride 2 × 5 min @ level 3 with 3 min @ level 1 between)	Rest	Ride @ level 2 for 40 min on a flat route (3 × 15-sec sprints mid-way with 5 min @ levels 1 and 2 between	Ride @ levels 1 and 2 for 180 min on a rolling route
Week 8	Ride @ level 2 for 40 min on a flat route	Rest	Ride @ level 2 for 60 min on a flat route	Rest	Ride @ level 2 for 60 min on a flat route	Rest	Ride @ levels 1 and 2 for 90 min on a hilly route
Week 9	Ride @ level 2 for 60 min on a flat route	Ride a hill-repeats session	Rest	Ride @ level 2 for 60 min on a hilly route (mid-way ride 3 hills @ level 3)	Rest	Ride @ level 2 for 60 min on a flat route	Ride @ levels 1 and 2 for 120 min on a hilly route
Week 10	Rest	Ride @ level 2 for 70 min on a hilly route, pushing to level 3 uphill	Ride @ level 2 for 60 min on a flat route	Ride @ level 2 for 70 min (mid-way ride 20 min at upper tempo)	Rest	Ride @ level 2 for 60 min (mid-way ride 4 × 1-min hill repeats with 3 min @ level 1 between)	Ride @ levels 1 and 2 for 140 min on a hilly route
Week 11	Rest	Ride @ level 2 for 70 min on a hilly route (mid-way ride 4 hills @ level 3)	Ride @ level 2 for 60 min on a flat route	Ride @ level 3 for 75 min (mid-way ride 20 min at upper tempo)	Rest	Ride @ level 2 for 40 min on a flat route (3 × 15-sec sprints mid-way with 5 min @ level 2 between)	Ride @ level 2 for 180 min on a flat route
Week 12	Rest	Ride @ level 2 for 60 min on a flat route (3 × 15-sec sprints mid-ride with 5 min @ level 2 between	Rest	Ride @ levels 1 and 2 for 60 min on a flat route	Rest	Ride at level 1 for 40 min (3 × 15-sec sprints mid-way)	The event

004 : Sportive Training

On-Off Switches_

Warm up with 10 minutes of steady riding:

+ Stay firmly seated in the saddle, don't move your upper body, and pedal hard for 10 seconds.
+ Pedal easy for 20 seconds.
+ Repeat the 10 seconds hard and 20 seconds easy for 15 minutes.
+ Pedal easy for 5 minutes.
+ Do another 15 minutes, alternating 10 seconds hard and 20 seconds easy.

Intensity: Really commit to the 10 seconds hard, but don't overdo the first 5 minutes of each 15-minute section of this training session.

so further, on less fuel. Core strength also adds to efficiency because it allows you to put more power into the pedals, and it means that you won't tire, or even worse suffer from backache, which can prevent you from completing an event.

Long rides

These are the lynchpin of cyclosportive success. You don't have to do all that many, but they must be done, and there is an art to doing them. First though, how far and how many? For a 160km sportive your longest rides need to be around four hours. You will be able to complete a 160km sportive without doing them, so long as you have done some structured and progressive training, but long rides bring another dimension to your performance and experience on the day.

As for how many long rides you should do, two or three in a 12-week build-up to a 160km event is ideal. In addition, some of their effects can be duplicated in the rest of your training, by upping the amount of riding you do at level 2 each week, for example. Another way to simulate long rides is to do two shorter ones in a day, but upping the tempo. For example, one ride of 90 minutes and a second hour-long one later in the same day, with long stretches of each ridden at upper tempo pace simulates many of the effects of a four-hour ride.

You might find that double days suit you better, especially if you like to train most days. Because the thing with long rides is that you need to be well rested going into one, and you need ample time to recover from them. Back off the duration of your sessions with three days to go, take a day off

VO$_2$ max intervals_

These can be done on the road or a turbo trainer. If you use a turbo, limit the interval effort to three minutes. If on the road the intervals can be three, four or five minutes long. Stick to three minutes for uphill VO$_2$ max intervals, four or five if done on the flat.

+ Warm up for 15–20 minutes.
+ Ride hard for 3–5 minutes. These should be full-on efforts. For example, if you pick three minutes you should be really looking forward to the end of it by two. For five minutes the same should happen after four.
+ Ride easy for the same duration as the interval you have just done.
+ Repeat the full-on effort interval.
+ Ride easy as above.

Start with two full-on intervals and if you cope well with that increase by one interval each subsequent time you do this session, up to a maximum of six repeats of three minutes, five of four minutes and four of five minutes. Don't focus on the quantity of these intervals, only the quality of them.

Cyclosportive

+ Training plan for a 160km cyclosportive

	Monday	Tuesday	Wednesday	Thursday	Friday	Saturday	Sunday
Week 1	Ride @ level 2 for 75 min on a flat route	Ride @ level 2 for 60 min on a flat route	Ride @ level 2 for 75 min on a rolling route, upper tempo on uphill	Rest	Ride @ level 2 for 75 min on a flat route (mid-way 15 min @ upper tempo)	Rest	Ride @ levels 1 and 2 for 120 min on a flat route
Week 2	Rest	Ride @ level 2 for 75 min on a rolling route, level 3 uphill	Ride @ level 2 for 60 min on a flat route	Do the on–off switches session	Rest	Ride @ level 2 for 75 min on a rolling route (mid-way 20 min @ upper tempo)	Ride @ levels 1 and 2 for 150 min on a flat route
Week 3	Rest	Ride @ level 2 for 70 min on a rolling route, level 3 uphill using a gear slightly higher than comfortable	Ride @ level 2 for 75 min (2 × 15 min upper tempo mid-way)	Ride @ level 2 for 60 min on a flat route	Rest	Ride @ level 1 for 40 min on a flat route (3 × 15-sec sprints mid-way, 5 min @ level 1 between)	Long ride done as specified, try for 3.5 hr
Week 4	Ride @ level 1 for 40 min on a flat route	Rest	Ride @ level 2 for 60 min on a flat route	Ride @ level 2 for 60 min on a flat route	Rest	Warm up to level 2, then do 2 × VO2 max intervals, then ride easy for 15 min	Ride @ levels 1 and 2 for 120 min on a flat route
Week 5	Rest	Do the on–off switches session	Ride @ level 2 for 75 min on a rolling route, level 3 uphill using a gear slightly higher than comfortable	Rest	Warm up to level 2, then do one more VO2 max interval than last VO2 max session, then ride easy for 15 min	Rest	Ride @ levels 1 and 2 for 150 min on a rolling route, upper tempo uphill
Week 6	Rest	Ride @ level 2 for 60 min on a route with long hills, level 3 uphill to just above by top of each hill	Ride @ level 2 for 60 min on a flat route	Warm up to level 2, then do 3–4 × VO2 max intervals, then ride easy for 15 min	Rest	Ride @ level 2 for 60 min on a flat route	Ride @ levels 1 and 2 for 180 min on a rolling route

Sportive Training

	Monday	Tuesday	Wednesday	Thursday	Friday	Saturday	Sunday
Week 7	Rest	Ride @ level 2 for 75 min on a rolling route, level 3 uphill	Ride @ level 2 for 60 min on a flat route	Do the on–off switches session	Rest	Ride @ level 1 for 40 min on a flat route (3 × 15-sec sprints mid-way with 5 min @ level 1 between)	Long ride as specified. Try for 4 hr
Week 8	Ride @ level 1 for 40 min on a flat route	Rest	Ride @ level 2 for 75 min on a flat route	Turbo on–off switches	Rest	Warm up to level 2, then do one more VO2 max interval than last VO2 max session, then ride easy for 15 min	Ride @ levels 1 and 2 for 120 min on a rolling route
Week 9	Rest	Ride @ level 2 for 75 min on a rolling route, level 3 uphill	Ride @ level 2 for 60 min on a rolling route (mid-way ride 20 min @ upper tempo in a gear slightly higher than comfortable)	Rest	Ride @ level 2 for 75 min on a hilly route, level 3 uphill	Ride @ level 2 for 60 min on a flat route	Ride @ levels 1 and 2 for 180 min on a rolling route
Week 10	Ride @ level 1 for 40 min on a flat route	Rest	Ride @ level 2 for 75 min on a flat route	Ride @ level 2 for 75 min on a hilly route, level 3 uphill	Rest	Ride @ level 2 for 60 min (mid-way ride 5 × 1-min hill repeats with 3 min @ level 1 between)	Long ride as specified. Try for 4 hr
Week 11	Rest	Ride @ level 2 for 90 min on a hilly route, level three uphill	Ride @ level 2 for 75 min on a flat route	Ride @ level 2 for 60 min (mid-way ride 20 min at upper tempo in a gear slightly higher than feels comfortable)	Rest	Ride @ level 2 for 60 min (mid-way ride 6 × 1-min hill repeats with 3 min @ level 1 between)	Ride @ levels 1 and 2 for 180 min on a flat route
Week 12	Rest	Ride @ level 2 for 60 min (mid-way ride 4 × 1-min hill repeats with 3 min @ level 1 between)	Rest	Ride @ level 2 for 60 min on a flat route	Rest	Ride @ level 1 for 40 min on a flat route (3 × 15-sec sprints mid-ride with 5 min @ level 1 between	The event

training two days before (that's no training at all!), and do one hour of easy pedalling the day before is good preparation for a long ride. Forty minutes easy on the day after, a rest day then a longer easy session should follow. After that you should be able to get back into normal training.

The other thing about long rides is that to be truly effective it's no good doing them at a dawdling pace. Begin with 15 minutes of level 1 riding, but after that start pushing into the lower part of level 2 and higher on the hills. Drop back to level 1 for stretches of 5–10 minutes every half hour. This simulates what will happen when you ride in a group in the actual event. Take enough food and drink with you.

Supplementary training

There are some things you should do off your bike that can give you huge gains in performance on it. They are supplementary training that supports your cycling. They aren't alternatives to cycling, like the things we'll talk about that you can do when the weather is too bad to ride.

The most important supplementary training exercises are core strength and stretching ones, although strength training by using weights or your own body weight is also important and well worth doing. Strength training becomes crucial as you grow older. We've included a strength-training programme in chapter 7 (Going Further).

Core strengthening

If your core isn't strong, when your legs push down on the pedals they also lift your body slightly, which absorbs some of their energy. A strong core resists this tendency to lift by pulling your body down into the saddle, giving your legs a solid platform to push against. With a strong core all of your leg power goes into pushing the pedals. Imagine being seated on the floor with your back against something and pushing a heavy object away from you with your feet. If the object behind you is rock solid you will be able to give a much stronger push than if it's flimsy and moves. Your core muscles are extra important when climbing.

Case history_

Hannah Reynolds, who finished 10th in the 2010 La Marmotte in a time 1 hour and 20 minutes better than her previous best says: 'My training was very focused for La Marmotte, which is one reason why I had a good result, but my longest ride was only four hours. The event is much longer, but you are going downhill for a lot of it, so you don't need to ride for the same number of hours. What I did do, though, was go quite hard on my long rides. I did 20-minute blocks at upper tempo pace, separated by bits of easier riding.'

Your core muscles also provide a link between your arms and shoulders, and your legs. You use your upper body a lot when you climb. Well-conditioned, strong core muscles provide a strong link between your legs and arms so their power is all transferred to the pedals.

Strong core muscles help to preserve optimal spine alignment. If there is one injury problem that cyclists tend to suffer from it is lower-back pain. This is because some of the prime movers in cycling are two large muscles located at the base of your back. Problems arise because these muscles are developed by cycling, so they become stronger compared to other core muscles and can pull your spine out of line, causing pain. Strengthening the rest of your core muscles counteracts this pulling, keeping your spine in its natural line.

To understand core muscles and how they work, think of your body from below your ribs downwards to the boniest part of your hips. Basically your core muscles form a multi-layered girdle around this part of your body, which is capable of moving your body in any direction: twisting, bending or a combination of both.

Core muscles do this because they are orientated in many different directions, so to strengthen them you must exercise them in many different directions. The best way to do this is by using a Swiss ball. These are sold online or in sports shops. It's important to get the correct one for your height, but advice is readily available on this.

The following is a core-strengthening routine using a combination of Swiss ball and free exercises. It takes 15 minutes at the most, and should be performed two or three times a week. You can do it at any time of the day. Follow the manufacturer's recommendations regarding inflating the ball. If you have difficulty performing the exercises let a little air out of the ball, as this makes them slightly easier. When you get stronger and better at the exercises you can inflate the ball again. And remember, these exercises are only effective if you maintain proper form while doing them; never sacrifice form to do another repetition. They must all be done slowly and with control. To make the exercises progressive just add on repetitions as you get stronger.

The reason why Swiss balls are so effective is because you cannot isolate just one core muscle group when exercising on them. For example, the exercises we've given you each focus on a particular core group, but the other core groups all work to preserve stability on the ball while you do each exercise. That's why one of the things to focus on for each exercise should be keeping the ball still.

You also need an exercise mat, or something similar, to perform some of the moves.

+ **Ball crunch**

Lie on the ball with your feet on the floor, hands either side of your ears. Pull your tummy in and roll your upper torso upwards. Focus on keeping the ball still. You need roll forwards only a few centimetres. Then lower your torso back to the first position slowly and with control. Repeat 10 times to start with.

+ Ball bridge

Start the exercise like the ball crunch (*see* above), with your lower back on the ball, then walk your feet out, so effectively you walk your upper body along the ball until you rest on it with your upper back and the ball is between your shoulder blades. Your arms just sort of hang naturally by your side. Lower your hips towards the floor then raise them again, holding the top position for two seconds. Repeat 10 times to start with.

+ Boxer crunch

This is like the ball crunch except you introduce rotation as you raise your torso. So rotate left to right first, then right to left. Focus on keeping the ball still. Start with five repetitions on either side.

+ Side raise

Lie on your side on your exercise mat with your shoulder supported by your elbow, and forearm pointing forwards at 90 degrees to the line of your body, feet together, one on top of the other. Raise your hips upwards until your body forms a straight line from your feet to your head. Hold this position for as long as you can. Then lower your hips with control. Repeat once each side. Do not hold the raised position longer on one side than on the other, even if you can. That will cause imbalances. If you find one side is stronger than the other, do the weak side first and only hold the strong side for the same length of time.

+ The plank

Lie on your front with both elbows supporting your shoulders, forearms together. Raise your hips until they form a straight line between your feet and head. Hold this position for as long as you can. Don't sag and don't raise your hips above the line between your feet and head.

+ Hamstring raise

Lie on your back with your feet on the Swiss ball. Slowly raise your hips from the floor, but as you do imagine you are lifting your back bone up bit by bit from the bottom upwards, like lifting a string of pearls. Focus on keeping the ball still.

+ Trunk raise

Lie on your back with your knees bent at 90 degrees and feet on the floor. Slowly curl your hips off the floor and towards your head, keeping your knees bent. Lower your hips with control and repeat 10 times to start with.

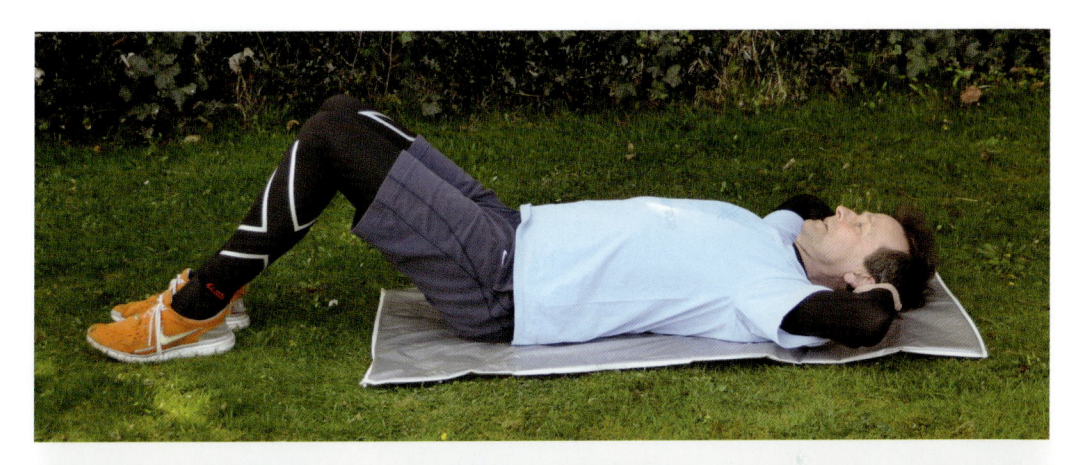

+ Side to sides

Lie on your back with your knees bent at 90 degrees and feet on the floor. Bring your legs up, with knees still bent at 90 degrees, until your thighs are at 90 degrees to your torso. Lower your legs to the floor on your left side. Keep your knees bent at 90 degrees and lower with control, as far as you can without your opposite shoulder coming off the floor. Raise your legs back to the start position and lower them to the right. Lift your legs back up to the start position and repeat a total of five times each side.

Stretching

Stretching does three things: it helps avoid postural problems that can be caused by cycling; it helps muscles recover; and it preserves their condition by preventing them from shortening, which they tend to do when worked hard.

Postural problems occur mainly around the shoulders and are due to a shortening of the front shoulder and chest muscles due to the way cyclists crouch over their handlebars. Your back and legs also require stretches because the prime-mover muscles in them can affect spinal and knee alignment, although core-strength training helps prevent this too.

Stretching after exercise helps muscles recover because it squeezes waste products and excess fluid from them. Stretching also guards against the tendency for hard-worked muscles to shorten.

You only need do a few stretches, and they can be done any time during the day, but just after a tough training session is the best time to do them. Never stretch a cold muscle though. And always release the stretch if it hurts or feels uncomfortable. The watchword with stretching is 'gentle'.

+ Quadriceps stretch

Lie on your side and bring the heel of your upper leg towards your buttocks. Take hold of it with your upper hand and pull your heel further towards your buttocks. Hold for 30 seconds, turn over and repeat with the other leg.

Cyclosportive_

+ Hamstring stretch

Sit on the floor with your legs stretched out in front of you. Place the palms of your hands on your knees and slowly bend your upper body forwards, trying to reach as far down your leg as possible with your fingers. Ideally you should be able to touch your toes, but just go as far as you can. Hold for 30 seconds and come back to sitting.

+ Chest stretch

Stand up straight with your hands clasped behind your back and arms straight. Slowly bend your upper body forwards and try to raise your arms away from your lower back. Hold for 30 seconds and slowly return to standing.

+ Upper-back stretch

Stand up straight with your hands clasped together in front of you and arms straight. Push your hands forward while trying to imagine you are pulling your shoulder blades apart. Hold for 30 seconds then slowly release the stretch.

+ Hip stretch

Kneel on the floor with your Swiss ball in front of you. Bring one leg forwards with your knee bent at 90 degrees and place your foot on the floor. Lean into the ball until you feel a stretch at the top and front of your kneeling thigh. Hold for 30 seconds, slowly release and repeat the stretch with your other leg.

The bricks

If you think about preparing for cyclosportives as being like building a house, the training you do determines its design and how big it will be. The bricks you need to build the house are the food you eat. If training is building, you can optimise it only by providing the correct raw materials. In the next chapter we talk about what you should eat to make the most of the training you do.

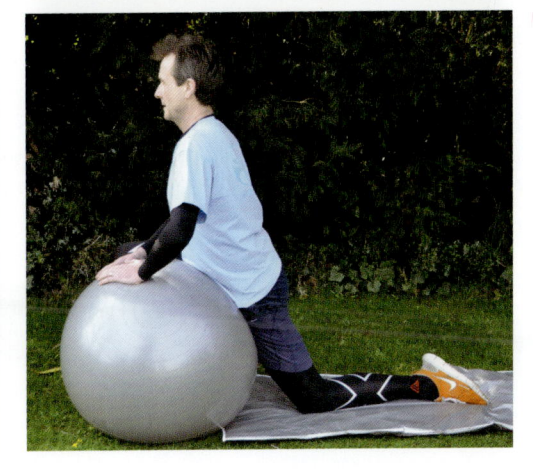

Case Study

British Cycling's top strength and conditioning coach explains why cyclists should consider doing some supplementary training: Mark Simpson

Mark works with some of British Cycling's top racers, including Sir Chris Hoy and Victoria Pendleton. Strength and conditioning coaches are trained to work on all physical and physiological aspects of an athlete's or sportsperson's training. That means cardiovascular training, aerobic speed, strength, power and injury prevention.

Mark's role with British Cycling is concerned with strength and power, and he assists with injury prevention and rehabilitation. He tends to work with riders in the sprint and BMX events, but he also works with endurance riders who have a particular need for speed, like in the sprints within a points race.

Even though cyclosportives are long endurance events, there is still a need for power and speed to underpin their endurance, especially if their ambition is a faster time. Cyclosportive riders also need strong core muscles and should stretch their muscle regularly.

'Strength training in the gym increases the amount of power you can apply to the pedals per pedal revolution. If you increase that then you will be able to accelerate quicker and climb faster. Strength training also impacts on everyday life. It helps maintain bone density, which is something cycling on its own doesn't necessarily do.

Anyone benefits from a strength training programme and it is very important in groups prone to osteoporosis. It also helps build and maintain muscle, and muscle burns calories 24/7, 365 days a year, so a strength programme can help with weight loss.

Core training makes you a better cyclist because the core is the link between five points of contact on your bike; those are two feet, two hands and the saddle. Think of them as a chain linked together by the core. If the core is weak they cannot work efficiently, no matter how strong they are individually.

Also, core training, along with improving flexibility, has an important general health role in that it mitigates against back problems and helps improve posture. Cycling alone can cause back problems because it causes tightness in the hip flexor muscles.

When muscles work hard they tend to shorten and that is felt as tightness. Cycling creates tightness in hip flexors, so stretching hip flexors is very important. The gluteal muscles also require a lot of attention.

Stretching doesn't only mitigate against problems of tightness, it improves a cyclist's posture, and will help him or her adopt and maintain a powerful, more aerodynamic riding position.'

004 : **Sportive Training**

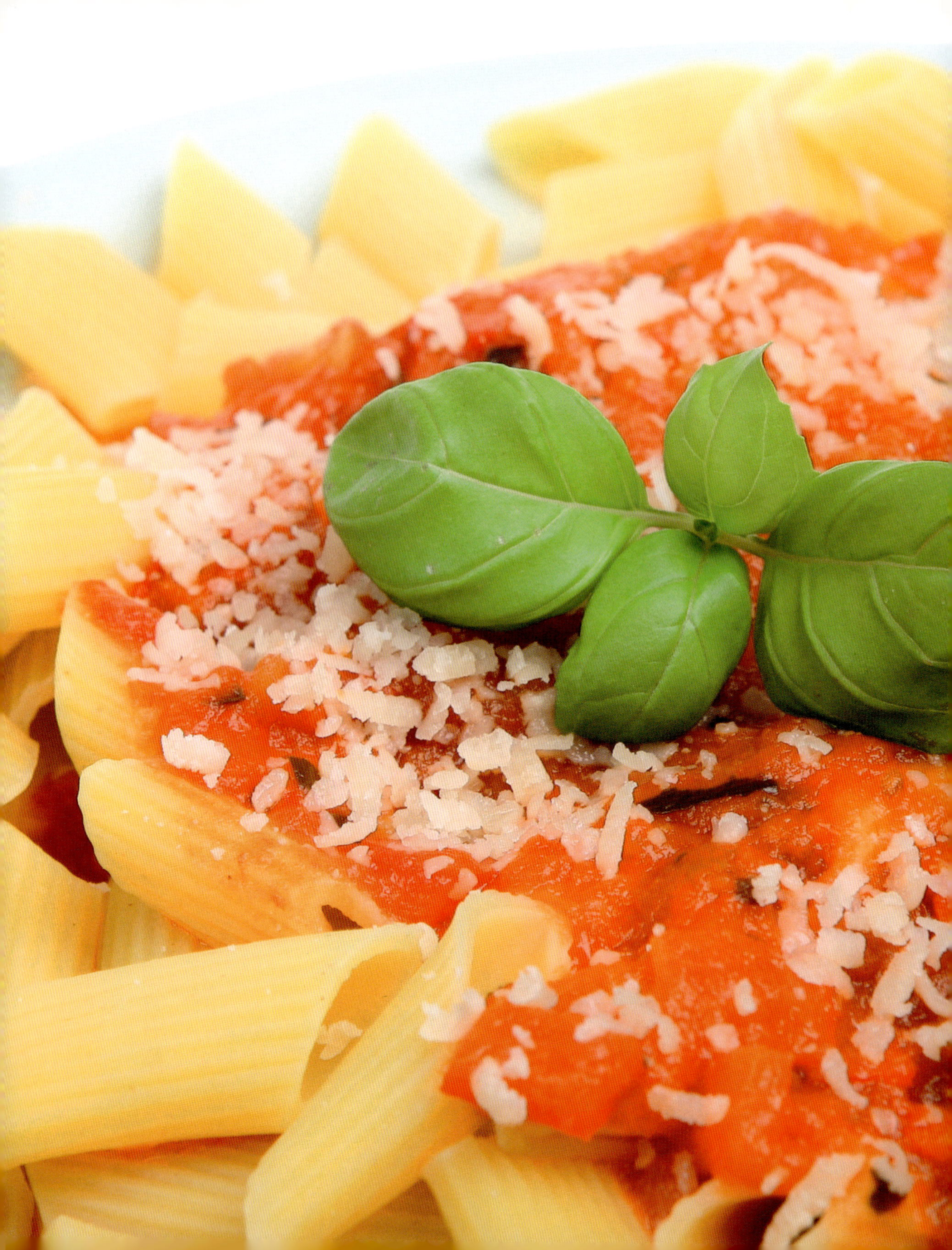

+ Sportive Nutrition
[chapter : 006]

The subject of nutrition splits into two: what to eat to support your training; and what to eat to provide fuel for energy used during an event. The two aren't entirely unrelated but they are different, so they require a different thought process and a different approach.

Broadly speaking, optimal training nutrition means eating and drinking the right things at the right time in order to support your training, and to recover from and assimilate the effects of it, while building or maintaining lean body mass. Event nutrition means eating and drinking to fuel the effort you are making there and then. So because it's more straightforward we'll deal with event nutrition first.

Event nutrition

This starts the day before an event, when you should eat what you would normally eat, but cut down on the amount of protein and increase the portions of carbohydrates you consume. Ideally these should be complex carbohydrates such as brown rice or wholegrain pasta (for a better definition of complex carbohydrates read the section on glycaemic index [GI] rating on p.xxx). Try to eat cooked vegetables rather than salads, especially during your evening meal. Limit the amount of fruit you eat too, because fruits and raw salads can upset your stomach, especially if you are nervous about the event. And don't eat a big meal late in the evening.

The big thing about pre-event-day food is it should be easy to digest, and it should top your energy supplies up to maximum ready for the next day. Cyclosportives tend to start early, which is why you shouldn't eat late, because digesting a late meal can prevent you sleeping.

However, if it happens that you can't eat until late then you must still eat. Cut protein down to a minimum, because it takes longer for your body to process; don't eat salad and instead concentrate on eating complex carbs. A full tank of fuel is more important than sleep.

Breakfast on event day is a very important meal, especially if the event is a long one. You might be nervous and find it difficult to focus on eating. Your nerves might also make you not want to eat, and in extreme cases some people find the thought of food nauseating. You have to fight these feelings and eat. Cereals with milk, yoghurt or fromage frais, and bread or toast with various spreads are ideal. Eggs are good, but bacon, sausage and other things in a traditional English breakfast won't help at all because they are too difficult to digest.

> **Pro tip_**
> 'One of the most popular pre-race meals that pro racers eat in the Tour de France is pasta, with olive oil, egg and a little bit of cheese grated on top of it.' Nigel Mitchell, nutritionist for the British cycling team and Team Sky.

105

Ideally, eat two hours before the event begins so digestion is well underway before you start and you won't have an uncomfortably full stomach when you get going. If you have to eat later than two hours before the start still do it, but cut the portion size.

You also need to go into your event well hydrated, so drink plenty of water during the day before, but not too much at one go. Also avoid things that work against good hydration. Coffee and tea have a diuretic effect, so limit yourself to two or three cups. Alcohol too dehydrates you, so while a glass or two of wine or beer will help you relax the evening before a sportive, any more than that will work against you. Avoid alcohol the night before if you aren't used to it. Drink a glass of water as soon as you wake on the morning of the event, and keep sipping plain water until the start.

Energy bars versus real food

A lot of science has gone into modern sports energy bars. Brands such as High Five, CNP, ZipVit and SiS employ specialist sports nutritionists who totally understand the demands of long-distance cycling. Many of the companies work or have worked closely with Tour de France racers to develop, refine and even invent new products. In short they work, and they will improve your performance.

On the other hand cakes taste nice, and they will broadly meet your energy demands during a cyclosportive. If you can't find an energy bar that you like or is palatable when exercising, cakes will do the job, only not as well. They provide a big burst of sugar, which can result in spikes and troughs of energy, whereas energy bars will drip-feed their energy into your system.

What to take with you_

Your event food and drink should be prepared the night before and put in a fridge. Take it to the start in a small bag then transfer the contents to the pockets in your top and bike just before the start. If you keep it all in one bag there's no danger of forgetting anything.

+ Two full-size bottles to carry on your bike, one with an energy drink diluted according to the manufacturer's instructions, and the other containing plain water
+ Energy bars
+ Real food, such as cakes if you prefer them
+ Energy gels
+ Two sachets of your chosen energy drink powder

Distribute the bars, cakes and gels evenly around the pockets of your top. Don't forget to put a mobile phone and some money in your pockets too, for emergencies.

Energy drinks, bars and gels often contain electrolyte minerals. These are crucial to your performance as they are responsible for the signals that keep your muscles going, and they help you stay alert and thinking clearly. Also, your muscles will cramp if you run short of electrolytes. The thing is though, the most important of these minerals when you are exercising – sodium and potassium – are lost through sweating. They need to be replaced, especially on hot days, and energy drinks and gels that contain them do so in amounts that are more speedily absorbed by your body.

+ **The case for cake**

You might argue that cakes would be better towards the end of an event, when you need energy fast, but energy gels are just as fast and they contain other vital nutrients, even performance enhancing ones like caffeine, and in a form where they are all easily and quickly absorbed. Gels are also very easy to use, you simply tear a portion of the top off and suck the contents down. No complicated unwrapping. And while I'm on about wrappers, you'll be tired, hot and bothered sometimes in an event or during a tough training session, but don't forget to put all wrappers back in your pocket and dispose of them in the proper way after the event or your training session is over.

To conclude the energy bars versus real-food debate, energy bars and gels do work best and you should choose them unless you really can't stomach them. However, there is one exception, which is best summed up in the following pro tip.

Pro tip_
'Keep something in your pocket that you really enjoy eating, and save it for when you go through a bad patch need to restore your morale.' Robert Millar – 1984 Tour de France 'King of the Mountains'.

Nutrition strategy

You need to fine-tune your own event nutrition strategy on your long rides, but here are some guidelines to start with:

+ Drink little and often, at least every 15–30 minutes depending on temperature.
+ Eat something solid after the first 30 minutes and repeat every 30 minutes after that.
+ Eat only half an energy bar at one go, unless the bars are small.
+ Start eating solid food, then progress to energy gels.
+ Drink a mouthful of plain water each time you eat.
+ Drink a mouthful of plain water after each energy gel.
+ Eat energy bars at the beginning of the event and gels towards the end.
+ If you feel your strength suddenly failing suck down a gel quickly, then eat something solid as soon as possible.
+ Some events offer energy drinks at aid stations, find out what it will be and try it out in training.
+ The sachets of energy drink you take with you should be mixed with water from an aid station as and when you need to replenish your energy-drink bottle.
+ Keep topping up your water-only bottle at aid stations.
+ Save something you really enjoy eating for when you need a bit of encouragement.

Hydration

Your body loses fluid through sweating and breathing. If you don't replace that fluid you cannot carry on working at the same rate. A 2 per cent drop in body weight through fluid loss impairs temperature regulation. A 3 per cent loss means reduced muscular endurance, and at 4 per cent muscular strength starts dropping. Then as internal temperature continues to rise the body begins to shut down as a safety mechanism. It is imperative to keep drinking.

Pro tip_
'I use a energy drinks, bars and gels, because I trust them to provide what I need to race. But I eat bananas in a race too. They provide a good punch of energy, plus they are one of the best sources of potassium you can find.' Dan Fleeman, pro racer and British national hill climb champion.

Your energy drink will meet some of these needs. In fact, it will meet more than just drinking plain water does because, due to the presence of other constituents such as carbs and electrolytes in it, it's absorbed by the body quicker than water.

The plain water you carry with you is for drinking when you eat or when you take a gel. In those situations the food or gel speeds up the absorption of both. Some energy bars contain electrolytes, which as well as being important for the reason we've discussed above, help speed up absorption of fluid in your stomach.

But plain water is also useful in hot conditions in another way. Yes, you must match the amount you drink to sweat loss, but plain water can help reduce sweat loss. The body loses heat by using it to evaporate sweat from your skin's surface. Pouring water over yourself conserves sweat by giving the body another liquid to evaporate and lose heat by doing it.

Pouring water over yourself in hot conditions also helps you maintain optimal power output.

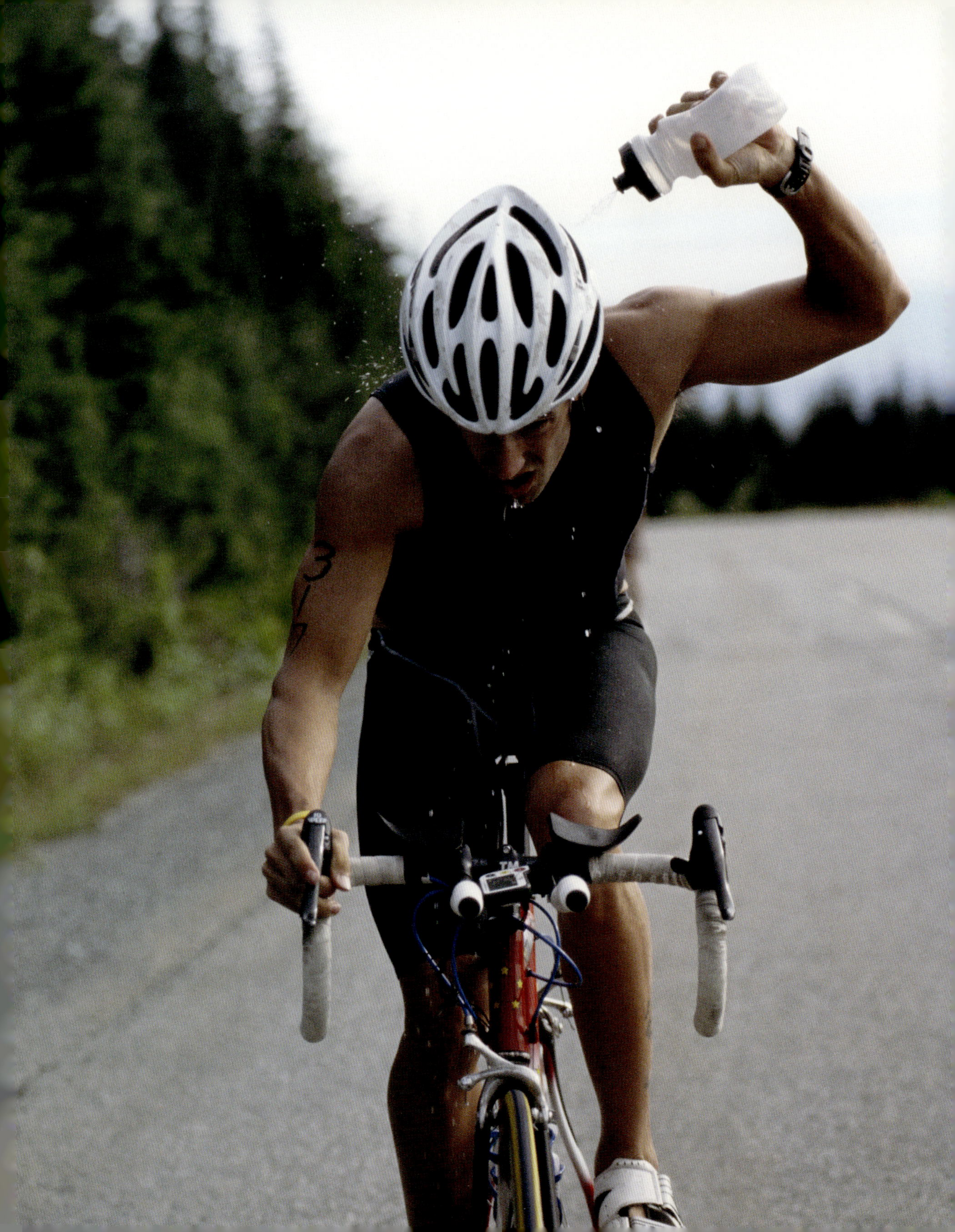

Your body loses heat by radiation as well as by evaporating sweat. Your blood carries heat to the skin's surface where it radiates away. But the blood diverted to do that isn't taking oxygen and nutrients to your working muscles, so your power output drops. Pouring water over yourself cools your body, so more blood goes to your muscles instead of your skin, taking nutrients and oxygen with it, so you can keep powering those pedals.

Afterwards

You might not feel like eating, but you probably will be thirsty. So after you finish the event drink a bottle of quite diluted energy drink, and make sure it's one that has electrolyte minerals in it. Don't gulp it down, take a few minutes to drink it.

As you get your breath back you need to think about getting some calories inside you to replace the energy you've just expended and to help your body recover. You need carbohydrates for energy, but the sooner you can get some protein for your body to use in repairing and rebuilding itself the better. But here's some good news: if you can eat carbs and proteins together in the first 30 minutes or so after you exercise they speed up the absorption of each other. This used to involve trying to eat a protein and carb sandwich when you still might be feeling a bit queasy from the effort you've just made, but now there are recovery drinks that provide carbs and protein in a palatable, easily digested mix.

Carry on sipping water for the rest of the day until you start urinating and your urine is clear. That's the sign that you are rehydrated. Don't be tempted to drink too much beer and wine after your effort to celebrate, as that sets your rehydration back. If you do get carried away and drink too much, your body is in no state to cope with a hangover. You will regret it, I promise.

If you follow these guidelines, within a couple of hours you will be well on your way to recovering from even the hardest event. To continue your recovery you should eat a proper meal, with protein, carbs and fats in it, plus some mixed salad, veg and/or fruits to continue getting the building

> **Cycling fact_**
> Cycling potential in its simplest form is expressed as an individual's power-to-weight ratio.

blocks of recovery as well as those essential vitamins and minerals inside you.

Training nutrition

Unlike for event nutrition, for training nutrition your strategy needs to be fixed as much in the future as it is in the present. What you eat and drink should support your training and provide the building blocks to help you not only recover from each training session but also build on the stimulus your training provides.

You therefore need to fuel your training and your recovery with enough essential nutrients so that your fitness improves progressively, while at the same time not adding extra weight to your frame in the form of stored fat.

Lose the fat

Your body produces power to push the pedals of your bike around. The more power you produce the faster you go. But there are other sides to the speed equation, and one of the most important is weight. If you can reduce your weight and produce the same power you will also go faster. Weight in cycling refers to you and your bike, but where your bike might weigh 10kg, you weigh a great deal more, so the potential for losing weight from your body is much greater.

Training correctly with good nutritional support will increase the power you can produce, and training specifically for cyclosportives increases the power you can generate over a long period of time. Now, if you can lose some fat as well you will be able to ride faster, particularly uphill.

While a certain percentage of body fat is required to maintain health, the rest of your body fat is a long-term food store, which does nothing to power your bike. That's the job of your muscles, organs and blood, as well as the bones your muscles are attached to. They all work together to power you along, but fat drags you back. You don't need it as a food store, that's a prehistoric adaptation dating from when we were hunter-gatherers and never knew when the next meal was coming from.

But losing body fat while maintaining muscle mass isn't easy, and it isn't something you can do quickly. Increasing the power side of your power-to-weight ratio brings bigger gains in speed anyway, so losing body fat isn't something you should get too hung up on. However, it's something to keep in the back of your mind, and it can be one of the side-effects of following the good day-to-day nutrition principles that support your training. It just requires a little manipulation, which will be explained later.

Food groups

This is just a quick look at the food groups that make up your diet, with a word or two about how they support your training. There are many books and internet sites that treat sports nutrition in a more in-depth way. What we've tried to do though is describe food groups and what constitutes a good diet for someone who want to take part in cyclosportive events. It's only a grounding, from which you'll be able to fine-tune your own diet as you gain more experience and more knowledge of what suits you.

+ Carbohydrates

These are grains, root vegetables, fruit and milk sugars plus other sugars. Carbohydrates are broken down into glycogen, which breaks down further into glucose when your body requires fuel. Glycogen is a half-way house in the carbs-to-glucose cycle, and it's stored in your muscles and liver. It's converted to glucose when your body needs it, such as when you exercise. Your body's glycogen stores are quite limited, which is why carbs are consumed on longer rides.

However, consumed carbohydrate that cannot be stored as glycogen is converted to fat, which is why you need to match your carbohydrate intake to the amount of exercise you do. Some carbohydrates are processed quickly, so their energy is available quickly. Some carbs are absorbed more slowly. The problem with the ones that are absorbed quickly is that if you don't need the energy they provide almost immediately, and your glycogen stores are full, they will be stored as fat. Because the slower-absorbed carbs release their energy more slowly there's more chance of your body needing it, so it won't be stored as fat.

This contrast is magnified by the fact that quickly absorbed carbs will leave you feeling hungry sooner than slower-absorbed ones, so you end up eating more. There's a handy measure called the glycaemic index (GI) for all foods. You can classify carbohydrates into low, medium or high GI by their GI value.

Broadly speaking you should restrict your carb intake to foods in the low-GI and to a lesser extent medium-G1 groups. The exception is when you are riding or immediately after exercise, when some high-G1 carbs will help fuel the work you are doing and will increase your rate of recovery from exercise because their quick absorption is beneficial then.

> **Tip_ Some useful advice**
>
> Keep these points in the back of your mind:
>
> + Become food and body-weight conscious, without becoming obsessed.
> + Make a note in your training diary of the food you have eaten and your weight, and look for correlations with how your training is going, how you feel and how well you are riding.
>
> But:
>
> + Don't become food and weight obsessed.
> + Do become food, weight and performance conscious.

+ Examples of low, moderate and high glycaemia index foods

GI rating	GI range	Examples
Low	55 or less	Most fruits and veg, pulses, whole grains, oats, nuts and fructose
Medium	56–69	Whole wheat, Basmati rice, sweet potatoes
High	70 plus	Baked potato, white bread, white rice, added-sugar or refined breakfast cereals, refined pasta

You should also try to match your carb intake to how much you exercise each day. Eat fewer carbs on light training days or rest days, and more before, during and after hard or long training sessions.

In the long term low GI carbs will help you lose fat while maintaining muscle. A recent research study of more than 900 adults and 800 children from eight European countries found that after six months, those on a low GI diet were on average 2kg lighter than those on rival diets with a high glycaemic index.

One very important fact to remember is that eating protein or fats with any carbohydrate lowers its GI number.

It's also a good idea to spread your carb portions over the whole day. Eat less at one go but eat a snack between meals. This drip-feeds you with energy all day. Include a small amount of protein with each snack, as it's also better to drip-feed proteins into your system throughout the day. This is because, like carbohydrates, your body needs only a given amount of protein at any one time.

+ Proteins

Proteins are broken down by digestion into amino acids, which your body uses to build new proteins in the form of body tissue such as muscles. Muscle fibres get damaged during training, but training sends messages that form little blueprints telling the body where to rebuild muscle fibres. This building won't take place unless you eat adequate amounts of protein.

Opinions differ on what is an adequate amount, but for someone training for tough events such as cyclosportives, 1g protein per 1kg body weight is considered a minimum to aim at, with 1.5g per 1kg necessary on really hard training days.

Again, it is important to match your protein intake to the training you do, because protein that isn't used in repairing or building body tissue will be stored as fat. This fact is another reason why your protein intake should be spread throughout the day.

Eating proteins with each meal is also useful because of their satiating effect. Proteins, particularly those found in eggs and dairy products, make you feel full and can help stave off hunger pangs. This is very helpful if you are trying to lose weight.

Good protein sources for athletes are lean meat, low-fat dairy produce, fish, eggs, pulses, beans and nuts.

+ Fats

First of all don't be afraid of fats. Your body uses fat for fuel, and it needs certain fats to function. Some fats even make you healthier. The thing to be aware of is the distinction between good fats and bad fats. Bad fats are generally solid at room temperature. So they are the fats you see on meat, or in cheese and other dairy products. Good fats are liquid at room temperature, like olive oil.

Eating too much bad fat can cause health problems, like raising the levels of the sort of cholesterol (we'll call it 'bad cholesterol') in your blood that coats your blood vessels and can cause high blood pressure. Good fats though raise the levels of 'good cholesterol' in your blood, which mitigates against the effects of bad cholesterol. Exercise helps do that as well, which makes exercising and avoiding bad fats a double healthy-lifestyle hit.

But while it's a good idea to cut the amount of bad fats you eat, most people can increase the amount

---

Sources of good fats_

+ Fatty fish such as tuna and salmon
+ Nut and seed oils
+ Nuts and seeds
+ Olive oil

of good fats they eat with health benefits. Anyone taking part in strenuous exercise will also benefit from doing this, as good fats reduce inflammation in the body, helping to speed recovery. There's even some evidence that says certain fats, those in fish oils, help preserve muscle mass.

One thing that should be avoided by everyone is hydrogenated fat or oil, as it increases bad cholesterol. Hydrogenation is a process used in food production, so you won't find any hydrogenated substances in fresh food. However, this is not a warning against processed foods, because many processed food don't contain hydrogenated fats. Just read the labels.

+ Vitamins, minerals and micro-nutrients

Whole books have been written on this subject. Suffice it to say that vitamins, minerals and some micro-nutrients play vital roles in your physiology. Some, such as iron and B vitamins, are really important to anyone training for an endurance sport or challenge. However, supplements, with one or two exceptions described in chapter 7 (Going Further), should be taken only on medical advice where a deficiency has been diagnosed.

The best way to ensure you get adequate supplies of these essential nutrients is to eat a wide variety of fresh food. Different nutrients are found in all the main food groups but in different foods, everything from meat to leafy vegetables and fruit. That's why a varied diet is essential. Processing, and to a certain extent cooking, destroys some of these substances, which is why fresh foods are better.

The cyclosportive diet

This doesn't need to vary much from a general healthy diet:

+ Try to eat from each food group, that's carbs, protein and fat, at each meal.
+ Include lean meat, white fish and dairy at least once each every week.
+ Include oily fish, such as tuna, salmon and mackerel, at least once a week.
+ Try to eat five portions of fruit and/or veg a day, and more if you can. A portion is not one slice of orange by the way, it's the whole orange!
+ Include good fat food sources at least daily.
+ Match your carbohydrate and protein intake to the amount of training or work you do.

One way of ensuring you get a good mix of nutrients is to try to have a lot of different coloured foods on each plate you eat. Different coloured fruit and veg in particular contain different vitamins and minerals.

Don't under-fuel on days when you don't exercise. The pace of modern life is tough, and stress consumes calories and nutrients. Look after yourself. Cut portion sizes on non-exercise days but never miss a meal.

Never train on an empty stomach. To get the most from any training session you have to fuel it, otherwise you won't be able to train with enough intensity to stimulate your body into adapting and getting better. Even if you exercise early in the morning, eat something before the session. Your normal breakfast will fuel mid-morning training. And one of the mid-morning or afternoon snacks listed will help fuel a late afternoon or evening training session.

Consume a bottle of water during easy training sessions of one hour or less. Take an energy drink on harder sessions of less than an hour, and use energy drinks, bars, gels or anything else you like for longer rides. Always take one gel on every ride that is just there for emergencies if you run out of fuel, which in cycling slang is called 'bonking'. No sniggering – the term comes from the fact that the sensations felt when you run out of fuel on a bike ride happen so suddenly that it's like being hit over the head with a hammer, hence bonk!

Finally, eat five smaller meals instead of three big ones. A typical day's menu for someone taking part in cyclosportives should look like this:

+ Breakfast

Low-fat milk with natural muesli or porridge, wholegrain bread with low-fat cheese, an orange.

+ Mid-morning snack

Oatcakes spread with peanut butter.

+ Lunch

Wholegrain bread with lean meat or chicken, tuna steak in tomato sauce with vegetables.

+ Mid-afternoon snack

Protein flapjack.

+ Dinner

Stir-fried turkey with vegetables and wholegrain pasta; avocado salad with feta cheese and sugar peas.

Tools of the trade

That's your diet sorted out. You've got the tools to progress in sportive events now. You can carry on enjoying them, trying new events in new areas, or even in different countries. Cyclosportive is a great way of seeing the world and meeting like-minded people.

The only thing left to help you on your way is to talk a bit about how to look after your bike and do some simple jobs on it, which we've left until the last chapter so it's always easy to find. Before that though there's a chapter for more experienced sportivers and for those who want to get competitive.

Case Study

What Tour de France racers eat and drink: Nigel Mitchell

Every day for three weeks, racers in Tour de France face what you will face in a major cyclosportive, so knowing their nutrition strategy gives you something to base yours on. In this case study, British Cycling's nutritionist, and nutrition advisor to Team Sky, Nigel Mitchell takes you through the menu for a Team Sky rider during one day in the Tour de France.

'A good hydration plan is the foundation of getting through a race like the Tour, where it's likely that the riders will race in temperatures of 20-30 degrees every day. In that situation, if hydration is good, then everything else fits into place.

Our riders start the day with a visit to the team doctor to discuss how they are feeling, and to catch up with any injury or other problems he might be treating them for. He might give them a check over and while they are with him they pick up a dilute fruit drink and start sipping it.

The fruit doesn't play a specific nutrition role, it's just to make the drink taste nice, which means the riders are more likely to drink the water. If they drink early it gets them in the habit of sipping away all day.

Next is breakfast, and this is where hydration steps up a bit with a fruit juice mix that's full of electrolytes, particularly potassium which plays an important role in the body and is lost easily through sweating.

They eat cereals, some bread and pasta with some protein like eggs or cheese. Not meat because it's more difficult to digest. Protein is very important for Tour riders, and for anyone in heavy training, as it provides the building blocks for your body to adapt to training. Protein can be taken in the form of whey powders, but this is only a supplement. With every aspect of nutrition the first line should always be good food sources. Maximise those, and just use supplements as they are intended – for supplementation. A safety net if you like.

Between breakfast and the stage start we give the riders 1.5 litres of juice flavoured water and encourage them to keep sipping so they drink at least half of it. One of the key problems with the big stage races is that they are often run at the height of summer. Heat is a problem, and therefore electrolyte loss is significant. We add a product called Gatorlyte to this drink, which is a powder that contains electrolytes.

Once the stage starts, the riders drink one bottle of water and one of sports drink, a bottle being the standard race size, per hour if it's hot. They also take gels, which contain electrolytes as well as plenty of calories. For food they eat sports bars plus cooked rice cake. Cooked rice is great race food because it contains lots of easily digested and available carbohydrate, and lots of water.

After the stage they get a protein shake, which helps meet fluid needs and starts getting protein into them to help them recover. If we suspect they might be dehydrated we've got another electrolyte drink. We've used that in races where the temperature is 40 degrees every day, and everyone was OK.

They might eat an energy bar or two while they are waiting, but the evening meal is the main refuelling opportunity. They eat easily digested pasta, good quality protein sources like fat-free meat, or fish with salad or vegetables. I like to liquidise salad and veg so as not to overload their gut with fibre. They eat plenty, at least three courses including a desert, plus there's fruit and protein bars available all the time.'

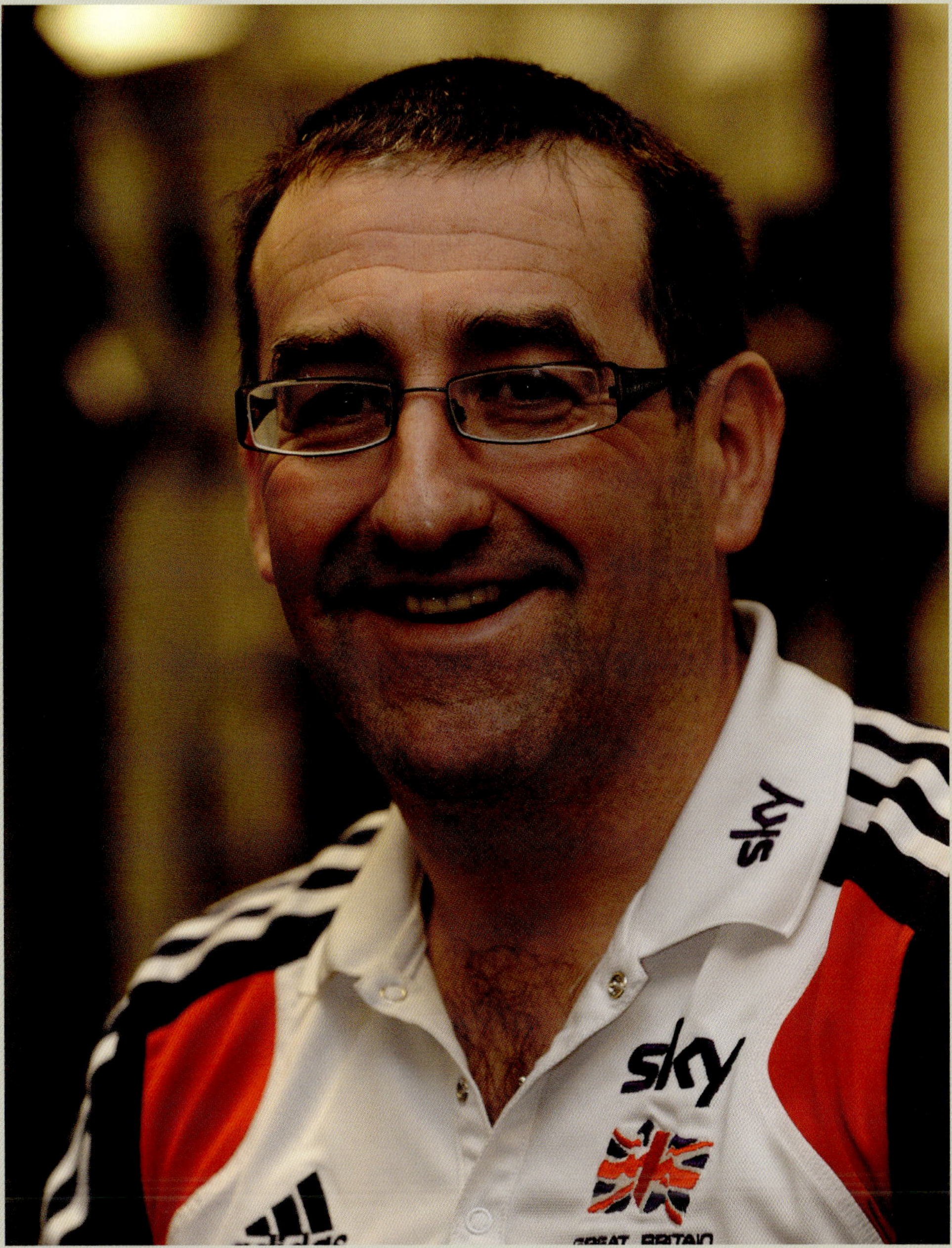
sky
sky
GREAT BRITAIN

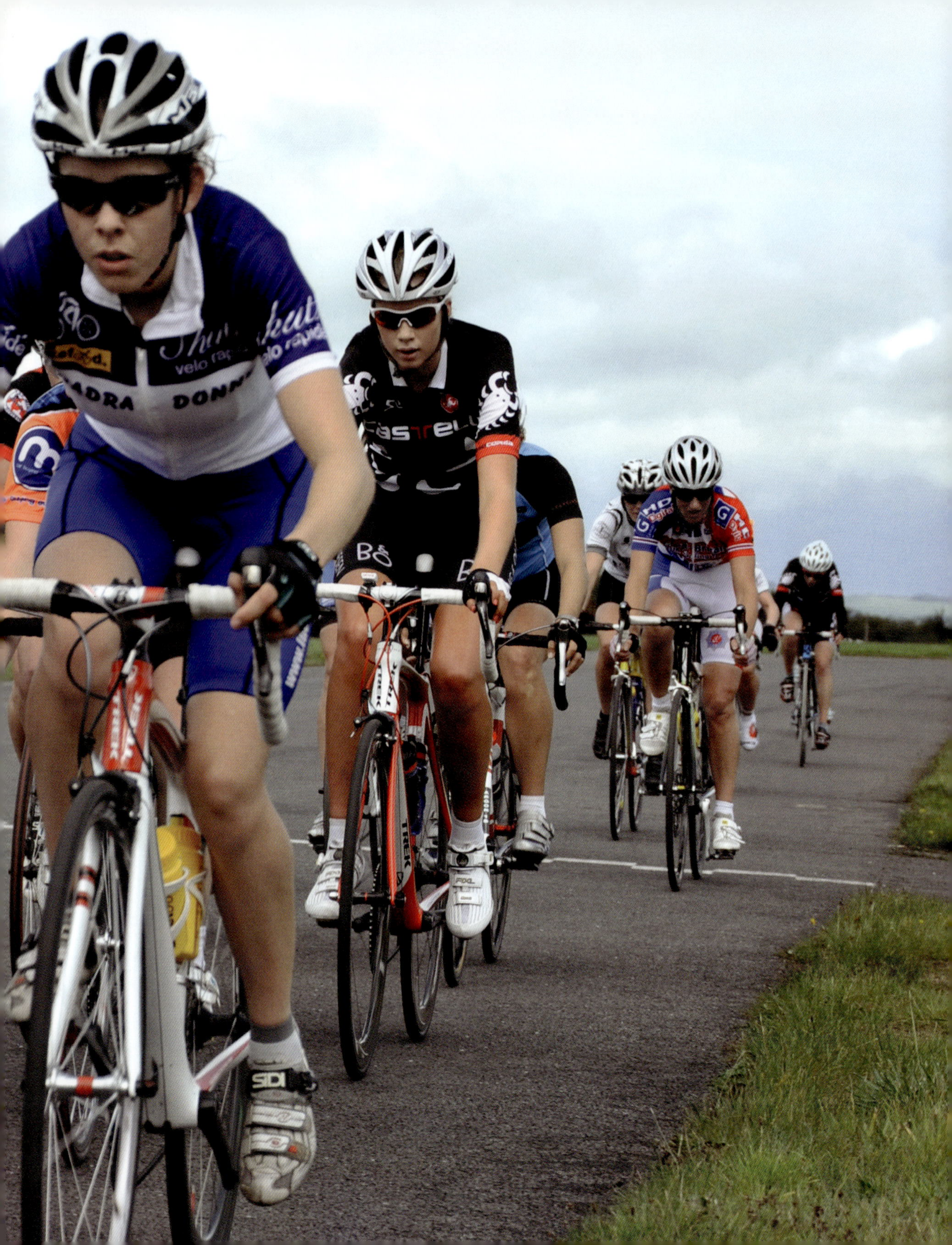
TREK
SIDI

+ Going Further
[chapter : 007]

You've got a few sportives under your belt; you're fitter, and you've seen there is a competitive side to them. If you have not been actually comparing yourself with other riders, then you may have been competing with yourself and against the course. Doing the same event again in a faster time provides a real sense of achievement.

Then there's the question of competing against other riders. You might have a bit of healthy rivalry going with a friend, or have your eye on a top-100, top-50 or even top-10 time. For older riders there is sometimes a separate list of times published per age group, as there is for men and for women. Progression like this is part of the challenge of cyclosportives.

Of course, you will improve if you have followed what has already been said in this book. Anyone who takes up anything new that involves a combination of self-knowledge, physical fitness, skill and experience, such as taking part in cyclosportives, can look forward to four or five years of natural progression.

However, there are ways of getting ahead of this progression curve, or at least working to enhance it. They involve looking again at how you train, emphasising different aspects of your training and learning new skills. You can also change the way you think about events, using mental skills to enhance your performance. You can even fine-tune your diet to give you significant performance gains.

Marginal gains_

The coaches who train British cyclists for the Olympics and other major competitions are some of the best in the world, as their athletes' phenomenal results indicate. They use a philosophy called 'marginal gains', in which they look at every aspect of the discipline the athlete is involved in, and at his or her training and lifestyle, and see if it can be improved in a way that will make them faster.

It doesn't matter how small a thing is: if it gives an advantage it's worth adopting. The idea being that a lot of 1 per cent gains add up. String 10 together and you produce a 10 per cent better racer.

Without becoming obsessed, adopting the marginal-gains approach to your cycling will make you a better rider. Bear it in mind when you read this chapter, and when you do anything connected with your bike. Read books and magazines, think about your cycling, and if something sounds logical try it. Remember to write it down in your diary though, and write down what effect it had.

Racing to improve

To do a faster time, to beat your rival and finish high up in your age group you have to ride faster, that's obvious. To get faster your emphasis in training should focus more on speed and power than riding long distances. You need to increase the amount of the genetic VO$_2$ max you can access, increase your threshold pace and increase your absolute power to become even more efficient. All these things will make you faster.

But boosting your speed isn't just so you can ride a faster time on your own. It's also to enable you take advantage of the group-riding dynamics that come into play at the front of cyclosportives. One important step you can take in this department is to take part in some road races.

Almost all over the world nowadays you will find entry-level or age-group road racing, in parks or on special bike-racing circuits. There's no better place to learn the art of riding in a group, making and following attacks, and working in breakaways. These are skills that you can use to your advantage in cyclosportives.

Group advantage

For the first sportives you do it's best to ride conservatively at the start and build up your momentum throughout the event. Riding conservatively is the best tactic for a first timer, but once you know your strengths, and you become a bit fitter, you can get a little more ambitious and think tactically. This is where road-race experience comes in.

There will be strong riders in any sportive who force the pace and cause splits. Quite rightly you ignored this before, but now you are more ambitious it could pay you to react to such moves and get into a the group that's pulling away from the rest.

You will need speed and power to do this, because such groups tend to leave the rest behind very quickly. Once the fast group are out of sight, their pace always settles down and you will feel more comfortable. However, the riders in such a group won't like it if you follow along at the back. You should go through the line and take your turn at pace setting at the front of it.

It sounds complicated but you'll soon see how breakaway groups form and work together. Watching bike racing on the TV will help you understand; so will taking part in some road races. It will also help you if you join a cycling club. These very often have coached group rides where road-race tactics are taught and practised.

Once you are in a fast group, even if you have to work hard when it's your turn to set the pace, you will gain from the collective efforts of the rest of the riders, which is in keeping with our over-riding philosophy of speed for free.

But never do more work at the front of any group than the average amount the rest are doing. Do even less if possible – you have to be a bit selfish

Case history_

Peta McSharry rode the Etape du Tour about three years ago, soon after she had taken up cycling. She says: 'I did some long rides to prepare and I managed it, just. I completed the course just inside the time limit. But I also found out that I really enjoyed cycling, so I started training harder and joined a cycling club.

'They got me into racing, and they changed my training so that I was doing a lot more interval training but fewer long rides. Last year I was 12th lady in the Etape, as well as finishing 15th in my age group at the world road-race championships. I reckon a lot of my improvement was down to being faster and stronger, but it was also due to the tactics I learned from road racing.'

in these situations. It's no good you doing powerful turns at the front, turns that pull the group away from those behind, and then exhausting yourself and getting dropped from it.

Try to stay with the group, even follow a further split if that happens. But don't panic if you get left behind by the others. You will have gained time from riding in the group, and other groups will have formed behind you. Ride conservatively, checking behind by looking over your shoulder and get in at the back of the next group that catches you. Stay at the back for a bit too. It's a funny thing but when a group catches a rider in a situation like this they don't immediately expect the rider to work with the group.

To get into these groups it's often necessary to ride really fast, sprinting and spending time at your VO_2 max, so that aspect of your training must be emphasised. Once a group is formed you will have to ride close to and above your one-hour power when leading it, so level 3 intensity also needs to feature in your training. This entails speed training for its own sake, not just to make you more efficient and increase your average speed as you did it before.

Later in the chapter we'll look at some more advanced speed and power sessions you can do, as well as threshold sessions. Before that though we need to visit an old friend.

Long rides revisited

Long rides still play an important part of your training if you want to become more competitive, but you don't need to ride further or do additional long sessions. Two four-hour rides in a 12-week build-up, with a few other longish sessions of 2–3 hours' riding at level 2 for some of the time, are all you need.

However, there is a way of doing your longest rides that will give you big gains, because it fully switches on the interleukin-6 response that we mentioned in chapter 4 (Sportive Demands). This is the adaptation to low glycogen levels that forces you to ride faster while using fats as fuel.

Be careful though, because these are not easy. Only one of your 4-hour rides in a 12-week build-up needs to be done like this. You should take sufficient food with you but don't over-eat. It's good to end these rides hungry, so don't eat anything during the final half hour, unless you feel you are about to bonk and run totally out of fuel. You must also stay well hydrated during the ride. Don't do long rides in too hot or cold conditions, and you must rest up before and after.

The way to do them is simple. Once you are warmed up push into low level 2, backing off to level 1 for

10 minutes after the first half hour. During the next half hour push through to upper level 2 by the end, before backing off for another 10 minutes of level 1. Repeat this low-level-2/upper-level-2-then-rest cycle for the rest of the ride, pushing to level 3 towards the end of the last half hour. You will be shattered, but it will be worth it.

These rides are quite stressful. They are meant to be simulations of a race-type effort, and you must treat them with respect. Eat and drink afterwards as though the session was a sportive event. But if you do everything about them wholeheartedly and with commitment, they will make you a stronger cyclist.

Strength training

Core-strength training is the most important training you can do away from your bike. However, if you are keen to improve you could well benefit from doing some general strength training, which will stimulate the production of the hormone testosterone, which plays a big role in your body's ability to build stronger muscle fibres. Such

> **Fast-twitch loss_**
>
> Nerves that stimulate fast-twitch muscle fibres tend to die before those that cause slow-twitch fibres to fire. This is why older cyclists should include speed training in their programmes, even doing full-on sprints as part of other rides. If you are over 40 get into the habit of doing two full-on sprints after warming up and before the main part of all your hard training sessions. You need all the muscle fibres you can recruit if you are going for a result in a cyclosportive, even fast-twitch ones because they add to the peak power you can produce – something you need on steep hills or if a group is forming that you want to be with. This really is a case of use it or lose it.

> **Cycling fact_**
> Training that provokes a response in the muscles to grow stronger doesn't stimulate the growth of extra muscle fibres. You have a finite number of fibres, so what the stimulus does is cause your existing fibres to become stronger.

strength training is especially important if you are a woman or a man over 40 because women produce less testosterone than men, and the amount of testosterone produced by men begins to fall once they pass 40.

Strength training combats this in two ways. It stimulates the body to produce testosterone, and it directly stimulates the production of stronger muscle fibres. It also plays a huge part in another factor that can rob older people of muscle. As you get older the nerves that command muscles to contract and relax tend to die off, unless they are stimulated. And if enough nerves die, so does the muscle fibre they are connected to. And they don't come back. Strength training, especially lifting heavy weights, keeps these nerves firing.

Strength training, particularly with weights, is something that requires specialist equipment and qualified instruction. Most commercial gyms offer both. Tell the fitness instructor that you are a cyclist and you want to be shown how to do the following exercises:

+ Leg press
+ Front squat
+ Back squat
+ Dead lift

These exercises can help you build the prime mover muscles in cycling. Focus on them and use them to create a progressive programme where you reduce the number of exercises you do while increasing the weight lifted per repetition.

Learn how each exercise should be done, and rigorously maintain good technique. Once you have each exercise down start training with 10 repetitions, and progress by increasing the weight lifted while reducing the number of lifts.

Training like this builds bomb-proof strength and power in your legs. Fit a progressive-weight training programme into each winter. Older riders should also fit a shorter programme in between each 12-week build-up to a cyclosportive. Everyone should try to do a gym session using at least one of these exercises and quite heavy weights each week to maintain gains.

Conditioning exercises

These are for your upper body, and you should take a different approach with them. You don't want to build muscles in your upper body, just condition them. These exercises can also help guard against 'round shoulders' and other postural problems that can occur to cyclists. They help keep your rib cage and shoulders open, which helps your breathing. Useful conditioning exercises include:

+ Upper body exercises
+ Bench press
+ Bent-over row
+ Shoulder fly
+ Good morning exercise

Cycling fact_
Cycling isn't a load-bearing exercise, and if it has one drawback from a 'promoting good health' angle, that's it. It is excellent exercise in every other aspect, but the bike carries your body, so your bones aren't put under a load, which means they don't get the stimulus that load-bearing exercise gives to maintain bone density. This isn't an issue for young people, but it becomes one as you grow older, particularly for women. Weight training is load bearing and provides your bones with all the stimulus they need.

Get a qualified trainer or fitness instructor to show you how to do each exercise. Do 3 sets of 10 repetitions of these exercises per session. To progress, build up the repetitions per set to 20 before adding weight. Use these exercises as part of your winter weights session, then include them once every two weeks during the spring and summer.

Home strength routine

There's another aspect of strength training that you can address with some simple home exercises, and that's targeting the smaller muscles that support the prime-mover muscles in your legs. These are muscles located deep in the back of your legs, your buttocks, around your knees and ankles, and in your lower back.

Treat the following exercises as core strengthening for your legs, and add them to your core-strengthening routine.

+ Step back

Stand on a step and step back with one leg until the lower knee almost touches the ground. Then push with both legs and slowly return the lower leg to the step. It is essential that you keep your upper body straight and upright for this. If you begin to lean forwards, that's a sign that the exercise has exhausted the muscles you are targeting, so it's time to stop. Aim for 10 repetitions with one leg, rest and switch to the other and do 10 on that. Never do more repetitions on one leg than the other.

+ One-legged squats

Place one leg behind you on something of about chair height. Place your hands by your sides, raise up on to your toes and squat down. Keep your body erect and try not to wobble. Return to standing using only the force of the leg you squat down on, again keep your body upright and prevent any wobbles. Aim for eight repetitions, rest then repeat using the other leg. If you begin to lean forward end the exercise.

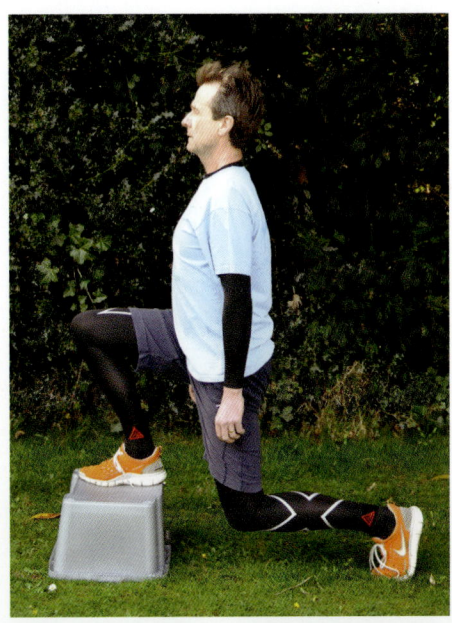

+ Step back

+ One-legged squats

007 : **Going Further**

+ One-legged flying

Stand on one leg and lean forward with your arms out like the wings of an aeroplane and put your other leg out straight behind you. Hold this position for 20–30 seconds without wobbling. Repeat using the other leg to stand on. When you can hold both sides perfectly still for 30 seconds, do it standing on your toes. And when you can do that without wobbling try closing your eyes to do it.

Planning your training

In chapter 5 (Sportive Training) we gave you some training plans or schedules to follow. Now though you should put your own training plan together. Still use 12 weeks of progressive training as your build-up to an event you are targeting. However, now you are more experienced you can include less important events or road races in each 12-week build-up, treating them as training sessions.

By now you will also know your weaknesses, and you should train to eradicate them. Weakness though isn't a nice word, so coaches prefer to use 'limiters', in that your weaknesses limit your potential. As a rule of thumb, bits of events that you don't enjoy or training sessions you don't like are often limiters. If you dread short climbs for example, it's probably a limiter for you.

There are some key training sessions in this chapter that you can use to improve your limiters. You should include them all in your training plan in any case, to increase your all-round strength and fitness for cyclosportives.

Once you have identified limiters and set about training to eradicate them, you can plan the rest of your training. The base of this will always be work at level 2 intensity, which you can either do on its own or combine with working at other intensities.

So over a year your training should go something like this.

Post-event rest

Take some time out after your final cyclosportive of the year to have a complete rest. And I mean rest. Two weeks of doing no exercise will allow your body and mind space to recover, and you will feel fresh when you start training gain.

Forming a plan

Don't do this during your down time, instead do it when you start a bit of casual riding again, just when you feel like it. Take two weeks to ride easy whenever you want or do any other form of exercise you like. During these two weeks analyse the previous few months. Look at your training diary, because it's an invaluable resource when planning ahead. You can see what training worked and what didn't, and maybe tally the times you felt good and not so good with the training you did.

Next think about the events you want to do in the coming months. You might not have the exact dates but most events stick to the same time of the year, so you can mark them down on your planner.

Count back 12 weeks from each of these events. If another comes within any 12-week period you have to decide which is the most important of the two or three and plan your 12-week training build-up for that, using the others as tough training sessions.

For each 12-week build-up use the plans in chapter 5 (Sportive Training) as a template. Then put in the training sessions you've identified that work for you. However, within each plan you must also include some that work on your one-hour power, your VO_2 max and your absolute power. That means riding at upper tempo, level 3, your VO_2 max and flat-out sprints.

You must also make each 12-week build-up progressive. So if you do three VO_2 max intervals in one session, in the next VO_2 max session try for four. Build up intensity and total volume over three weeks, then do an easier week. And rest up and recover fully from your long rides.

It's also important to follow hard sessions with an easier one. These don't have to be full recovery days where you rest totally, although you do need one or two total rest days a week. The pattern of rest day, hard day, easier day, hard day, rest day, short fast day, longer ride is a good one to follow over a seven-day period.

Once you have sorted out your target events and your 12-week build-ups, you will probably be some way off the beginning of the first one. This is what cyclists call the off-season, and in northern Europe it also coincides with cold, rainy and snowy winter.

The off-season

The winter is a good time to work on your general fitness. Then you can make that fitness more cycling-specific when the weather gets better from the end of winter and into spring.

To kick off your training during the winter, ride outside whenever the weather is good and you feel like it. Just make these enjoyable relaxed rides, where and whenever you want.

The focus of your training at the beginning of the off-season should be a 12-week strength training programme. After that try to do one session in the gym each week even in the summer, and older riders should definitely do this.

This is a good time of year to start running, if you enjoy running that is. It's a great cardio-vascular exercise that is convenient to do anywhere, and it has some direct crossover benefits for cyclists. Running up hills is particularly good. Buy some good running shoes from a specialist shop that will help you pick a pair to suit your feet.

I'm such a fan of running as a substitute for cycling that I'd encourage you to keep it up all year. It's a great way of getting a quality fitness session in if you can't ride your bike for some reason. If you are travelling, for work for example, and can't take your bike with you, running is something you can do with minimal equipment. Running is also a great help in controlling your weight. However, if you rely on running as a replacement for bike training during the cycling season, do a short session, just 20 minutes or so, every week, so your legs are always accustomed to it.

Getting serious

The end of the first month of the off-season is time to start bringing some discipline and direction to your on-the-bike training. Short sessions using a turbo trainer will help you do this. Pick a session from 'speed and power' and one from the 'upping your one-hour power', and do each one each week. Make these sessions progressive as the weeks go by.

Use the weekends to put in some longer rides in daylight. A good thing to do at this time of year is use your bike for adventure and do some rides in areas where you haven't been before. Adventure is good motivation to get out on cold days. A mountain bike is a great tool as it allows you to go off-road, where you can keep your wheels rolling safely even on days when the roads are a bit icy.

Keep to this pattern through the middle of winter, maybe trying to do a good steady road ride mid-week if you get the opportunity. Write what you do in your diary: record waking pulse, weight, how much you slept and how you feel, both in training and regarding your health. Reading back over your diary will ensure your training is progressive, and it will flag up any growing tiredness. Your diary is the resource that allows you to fine-tune your training.

Speed and power sessions

Here are three training sessions that will help you go with splits and survive the initial burst of speed that gets them established ahead of the rest.

Upping raw power

This can be done on a turbo trainer or on a hill.

+ Warm up thoroughly until you are riding at level 3 intensity.
+ Ride as hard as you can for 20 seconds in a much higher gear ratio than you would normally use.
+ Pedal very easily for 1 minute.
+ Repeat the 20 seconds hard, 1 minute easy for a total of 6 times, to a maximum of 10.
+ Ride very easy for 5 minutes.
+ Ride for the rest of the duration of the session (1 hour is a good total duration for this one) at low level 2, easing to level 1 towards the end.

One-minute intervals

This can be done on a turbo trainer or on a flat or rolling road.

+ Warm up as above.
+ Ride as hard as you can for 1 minute, but spread the intensity over the whole 60 seconds. It's no good doing the first 30 seconds hard and grovelling for the next 30.
+ Ride easy for 2 minutes.
+ Repeat the 1 minute hard, two minutes easy for a total of 5 times to begin with, working up to a maximum of 10.
+ For variation, occasionally cut the intervals to 30 seconds hard, 1 minute recovery, but go harder in the 30 seconds. Do the same total number of intervals – to 10 maximum.
+ Ride for the rest of the duration of the session (1 hour is a good total duration for this one) at low level 2, easing to level 1 towards the end.

> **Pro tip_**
> 'With the distance of some pro races you had to do some six-hour training sessions, and sometimes do them on consecutive days. If I did them on roads I knew I was looking at my watch, willing the time to pass. So I turned them into adventures by plotting routes to places I'd never ridden in before.' Olympic champion, world record holder and Tour de France yellow jersey Chris Boardman.

11:00
11:30
12:00
12:30
1:00
1:30
2:00

VO$_2$ max with a twist

This can be done on a turbo trainer or on a flat or rolling road.

+ Warm up as above.
+ Sprint for 15 seconds then continue riding at just above level 3 for 2 minutes 30 seconds, then sprint for 15 seconds.
+ Ride easy for 6 minutes.
+ Repeat the above sprint, level 3-plus, sprint once more.
+ Just do 2 of these repeats to start with and work up to a total of 4.
+ Ride for the rest of the duration of the session (1 hour is a good total duration for this one) at low level 2, easing to level 1 towards the end.

Upping your one-hour power

Here are some training ideas that will help you increase your ability to ride at a high average speed.

Long climbs

Ideally you should find a hill that takes at least 10 – preferably 20 – minutes to ride up. It doesn't have to be all uphill, just generally uphill trending terrain. You can also simulate long hills on a turbo trainer by raising the front wheel of your bike on a block, and if your turbo has that facility, upping the resistance on it.

+ Warm up thoroughly and ride your hill at level 3 all the way.
+ If it's a 20-minute hill do this once, if it's a 10-minute climb do it twice. If it's in between 10 and 20, ride up the second time only until the total at level 3 adds up to 20 minutes.
+ Ride easy for the rest of the session.

Sixteen-kilometre time trials

These are organised by cycling clubs throughout the country. Often they are quite informal evening events, where for a small fee anyone can ride. Some are official races that require you to be a member of a club. They are great for increasing your one-hour power, because 16km is a distance at which you can ride at just above your one-hour intensity level. Competition is also a good spur. If there are no races near you create your own course, either approximately 16km around, or 8km out and 8km back along the same road. Stick to the same course and put the times in your diary so you can compare times to see if you are progressing.

+ Warm up well before the time trial, and ride easy for about 15 minutes in a low gear afterwards.

Three-minute steps

This is a great session for improving your pedalling action and efficiency, your strength and your one-hour power. You can do it on the road or on a turbo trainer.

+ Warm up until you are riding at level 3.
+ Shift your chain on to the big chainring and second largest sprocket. Ride hard in this gear ratio for three minutes.
+ Ride easy for one minute.
+ Shift to your large chainring and third largest sprocket. Ride hard in this gear ratio for three minutes.

- Ride easy for one minute.
- Shift to your large chainring and fourth largest sprocket. Ride hard in this gear ratio for three minutes.
- Ride easy for one minute.
- Shift to your large chainring and fifth largest sprocket. Ride hard in this gear ratio for three minutes.
- Ride easy for one minute.
- Shift to your large chainring and sixth largest sprocket. Ride hard in this gear ratio for three minutes.
- You should see your speed increase for each of these three-minute intervals.
- Once you have completed five intervals in total, ride easy for the remainder of the session.

Nutritional support

Training harder won't work unless you supply your body with the building blocks it needs to get fitter and stronger. You must also factor in enough rest to allow the building process to occur. The harder you train the more quality nutrition and quality rest become important. Pro cyclists are legendary at resting. Try to get eight hours' sleep at night, because when you sleep your body produces more human growth hormone, which helps your muscles build and recover. It's also been discovered that the most growth hormone is secreted just after you fall asleep, so a daytime nap can provide an additional burst of hormone, bringing about speedier recovery.

You don't have to do anything dramatic or make huge changes. Just follow these principles:

- Stay hydrated throughout the day by drinking 2–3 litres water over each 24-hour period.
- Put as many different coloured foods on your plate as you can.
- Eat a balanced diet of all the food groups, with plenty of fruit and vegetables.
- Eliminate junk food as much as possible.
- Cut down 'bad' (saturated) fats.
- Increase the amount of 'good' (unsaturated) fats you eat.
- Try for 1.5g protein per 1kg body weight on hard training days.

> **Pro tip_**
> 'There's an old saying in pro cycling, but it's a true one. As you go about your normal day and you find yourself standing still you should sit down, and if you can sit down you should lie down.' Barry Hoban, winner of eight stages in the Tour de France.

- Try to eat carbohydrates from the low and medium GI group (see p.xxx).
- Match your carb intake to the amount of work you do.
- Weigh yourself once a week to see if weight is creeping on. Remember, what gets measured gets managed; scales are your best friend if you want to stay lean.
- Read a good sports nutrition book and follow its principles.

Supplements

There are some supplements that are worth considering when you are training hard.

Fish oil

This reduces inflammation, so can help you recover. It promotes vascular health, keeping all-important blood vessels in good working order. There is also evidence that fish oils may be able to increase your training capacity, so you can strain harder giving your body a bigger stimulus to get stronger and fitter. Fish oils also contain zinc and magnesium, which can increase the production of testosterone. This promotes muscle rebuilding.

Protein supplements

Whey protein powder that you can mix into a shake provides a quickly digested source of protein, and so helps your body rebuild. It also reduces hunger, so is useful if you are trying to lose weight. Timing with protein supplements is important. Because it is quickly digested, whey is best taken immediately after exercise or in the morning. Later in that day it's best to take a supplement that blends whey with a much slower-acting protein, caesin. Such supplements work because whey switches on protein synthesis in your body, then caesin provides another shot of protein for your body to build with.

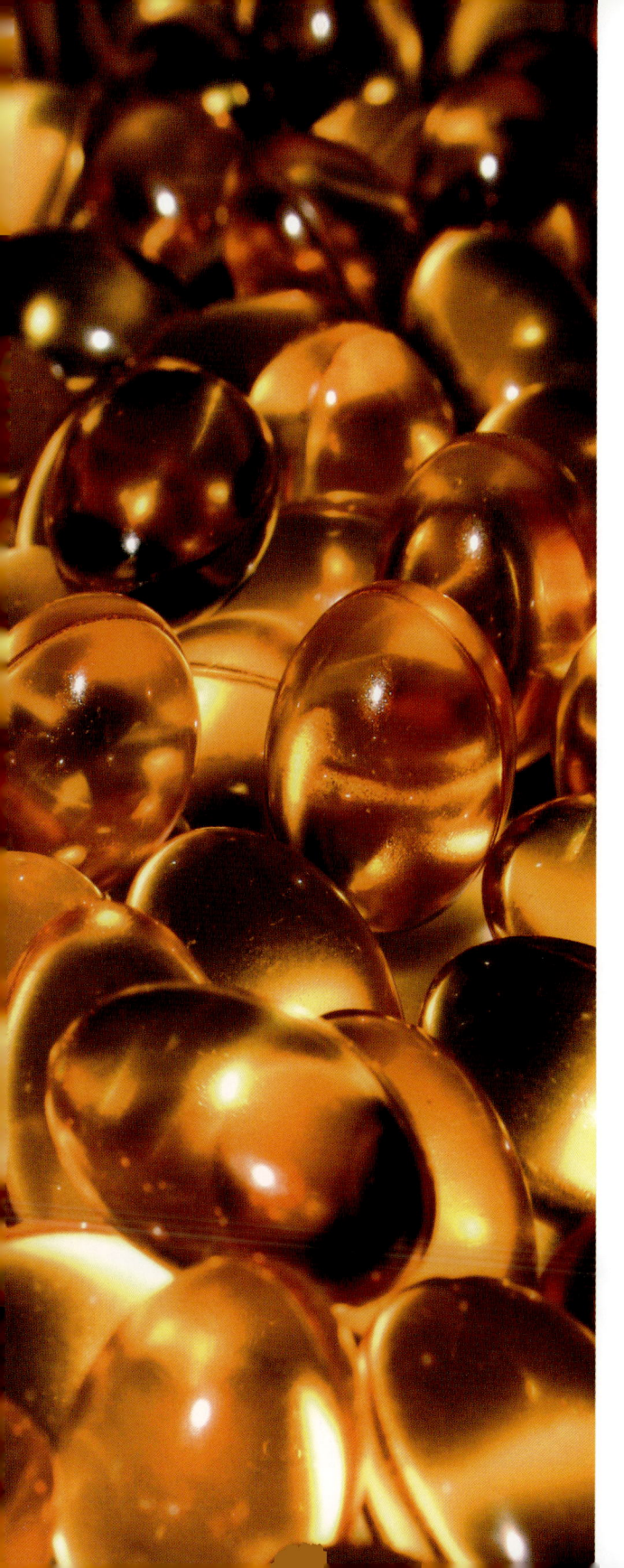

Conjugated Linoleic Acid (CLA)

This is a fatty acid found in meat and cheese that is thought to prevent weight gain. You can buy it in capsule form.

Keep on pushing

Other supplements and other ways of training are always being discovered, and it pays to keep up with what's going on by reading cycling magazines. You can also learn from other sports. Incorporating tweaks and marginal gains will make you a better cyclist, but don't lose sight of the principles.

Work on your efficiency, your power, your VO_2 max and one-hour power. Do the long rides. Eat and rest well. Add the tactics and experiences into the mix that you'll learn from taking part and from other cyclists you meet. Keep the speed-for-free mantra in your head, too, and add another; you only get out of cyclosportives what you put into them. They are a real sporting leveller, where hard work means more than talent. Enjoy!

Case Study

A Team Sky professional talks about training to meet his big challenge: Russell Downing

Russell Downing, 32, is a member of one of the most highly organised and well funded teams in pro-bike racing. However, he hasn't always been in this position. Downing has wanted to be a pro-racer since he was a boy, but bad luck, and a couple of wrong choices kept him out of the top flight until a couple of years ago.

He had the ability and he'd always won races too, but he needed to win consistently at the highest level to get where he is today. The thing is, in the relatively small teams he was in, he didn't often get chance to compete against the big boys. So, when he did he had to make it count.

'I knew I could ride well at the top level, but to prove it I had to do well in top level races. But I was in a bit of a Catch 22 situation. You need to ride big races to get the form to win big races, and in particular you must ride big stage races, but I didn't get to ride that many.

I trained by doing a lots of the things Chris recommends in this book. I did long rides, I rode with a fast training group, made big efforts on hills, did intervals, and of course I raced. It's no good just doing long rides if you want to get really fit; you have to train all the energy-producing processes in your body. But the thing is, before I got into Team Sky I didn't ride the kind of races I needed to regularly to get the form to win one, so I used to simulate these stage races in training.

I'd do long rides, sometimes one day after another for up to six days, to simulate stage races. I'd even change my eating pattern so that I was eating like I would in a stage race. I also used some races as training. I'd ride hard the day before and the day after so the race was part of a block of training.

It worked. By simulating top-level stage races I got the form to finish second in the 2008 Tour of Ireland against top opposition in big teams. And in 2009 I won it, even though most of my team couldn't help me because the race was above their level. I had to race virtually on my own against teams who'd just done the Tour de France. Even Lance Armstrong rode that race.

The win in Ireland confirmed my ability to Team Sky, so they offered me a place. In 2010 I won three big races for them, and now I've just completed my first Grand Tour, the Tour of Italy. What I'm saying is if you go that extra mile in training, push yourself extra hard. So long as you don't overdo it and you listen to your body, you can achieve what you want to achieve. The SAS have a motto: "train hard, fight easy", and those guys really have to achieve what they've set out to do or they get hurt or killed. It's not a bad motto for a cyclist to follow.'

007 : **Going Further**_

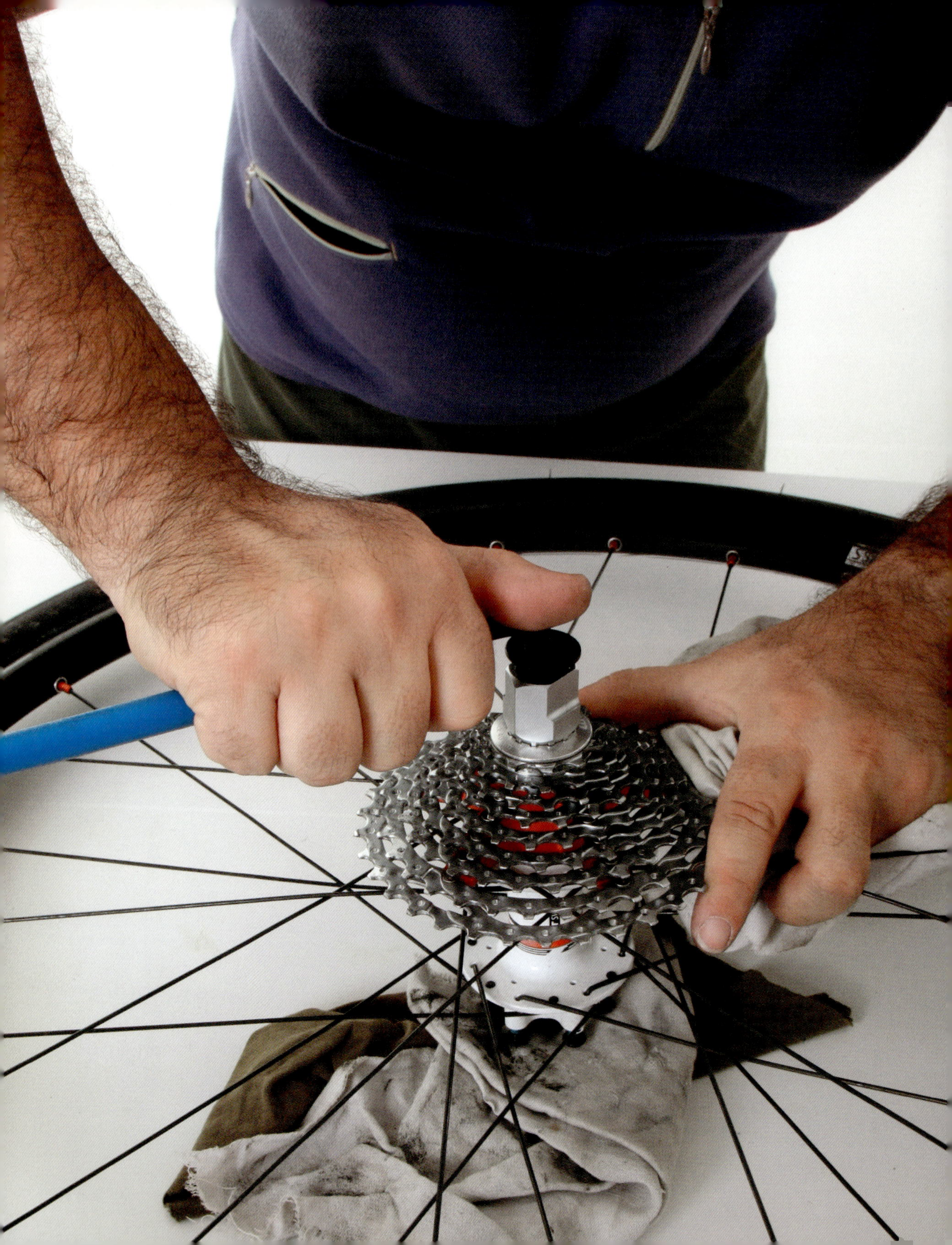

+ Bike Care

[chapter : 008]

Bike maintenance is a big subject, and one that's been covered by a number of very good books. If you don't know how to do basic adjustments to your bike then it's well worth buying such a book. It's also worth cultivating a working relationship with a good bike shop, and that means buying stuff off them from time to time. If you keep them happy they'll be there for you when last-minute mechanical disasters strike, and that's a resource well worth having.

In this chapter we show you some basics: how to clean your bike; how to carry out pre-ride safety checks; how to repair a puncture; and how to adjust your gears. It finishes off with a section that addresses some common bike-care questions.

Keeping your bike clean

Not only does a clean bike look better but it works better and lasts longer too. Road dirt and old lubricant act as a grinding paste, wearing out components fast. Also dirt hides stuff that might become a problem, such as cuts in tyres and chips in paint that might lead to corrosion.

You should clean your bike once a week, and after every wet ride. If you haven't time to do the whole thing, just clean the drive train, which is the chain, chainset and sprockets. You need some bits of kit to clean your bike:

+ Bucket of hot soapy water
+ Clean sponge
+ Degreaser spray
+ Dirty sponge
+ Dry cloths
+ Hose-pipe or other clean water for rinsing
+ Lubricant
+ Selection of different-sized, stiff-bristled brushes

Step 01

Remove the wheels and spray degreaser over the chain, and over the front and rear mechs. Allow the degreaser to soak in.

Cyclosportive_

Step 02

Wash off the degreaser with hot soapy water, using the dirty sponge you should keep just for this job.

Step 03

Clean both wheels with hot soapy water, using a stiff brush. Work the water in between the spokes and around the hubs. Scrub the tyres, and check for cuts.

Step 04

Wash the rest of the frame with hot soapy water, using sponges, cloths and different-sized brushes to get into hard-to-reach places. Start at the top of the frame and work down.

Step 05

Rinse the wheels and frame with clean water and dry them with a clean cloth. Reassemble the bike and check the frame for blemishes and wear.

Step 06

Lubricate all moving parts with a bike-specific lubricant.

Pre-ride checks

These don't take long, but doing a few pre-ride checks are essential for safety. Get into the habit of doing them before each ride. Also have a close look at the frame once a week, or whenever you clean your bike, which should be at least weekly. Use touch-up paint to cover up any chips in the frame. If you discover a crack, take the bike to a reputable bike shop for them to look at and advise.

Step 01

Fully apply your front and rear brakes while trying to push your bike forwards. Neither wheel should turn. Adjust the brake travel if they do. A bike shop will do this if you don't know how to. Inspect the cables inside brake levers for fraying. Replace if you see any. All the cables on your bike should be replaced once or twice a year.

Step 02

Hold the front wheel between your legs and try to turn the handlebars. They shouldn't move.

Cyclosportive_

Step 03

Lift the front of the bike and slowly turn the front wheel, inspecting the tyres for bulges, cuts or excessive wear. Repeat for the back wheel and replace the tyre if you see any defects. If either wheel touches the brake blocks then it isn't running true or the brakes need attention. A good bike shop will advise.

Step 04

Check that the quick-release levers on your wheels are in the locked position. Most have the words 'lock' and 'unlock' on them – 'lock' should be outermost. If yours don't have those words on them, get familiar with how they work and how they look when locked.

Bike Care

Step 05

Check that bottle cages, any bags, pump and saddle are secure.

Step 06

Check the gear shifts because if these aren't perfect they can distract you when riding, and having your chain slip out of gear can cause injury. So, with the rear wheel raised, run through all the gear shifts. If shifts aren't instant and smooth, or there is chain noise when running on a particular sprocket or chainring, the rear or front mech needs adjusting. If you bought your bike from new, instructions for this should come with it. We've also included some steps on how to adjust your gears in the following section.

145

Cyclosportive_

Repairing a puncture

You need:

+ Puncture repair kit containing glue, patches, a crayon marker, French chalk and some kind of abrasive surface
+ Three tyre levers
+ Tweezers

Step 01

Remove the wheel then insert the blunt end of a tyre lever between the tyre and wheel rim. Lever the edge of the tyre over the rim. With the lever still under the tyre, hook its other end around a spoke. Insert the second lever and push this around the tyre to lift it off, then remove the inner tube. If the tyre is tight you might need to hook the second tyre lever to a spoke and use a third one to remove the tyre.

Step 02

Lift the tyre completely off the wheel and inspect it inside and out for cuts and anything sticking through it. A deeply cut tyre needs replacing. Remove any objects sticking in the tyre by pulling them out from the outside. Tweezers are useful for this.

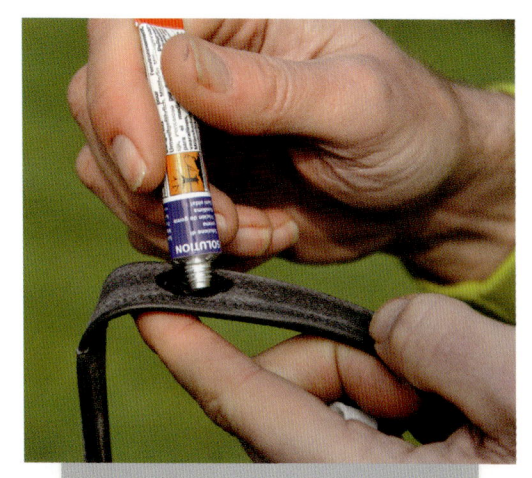

Step 03

Inflate the inner tube and listen for escaping air to locate the puncture. Mark where it is, then work around the whole tube listening in case of more holes. Deflate the tube and roughen its surface around each hole with abrasive. Select a repair patch and spread a thin layer of glue over the roughened area of the tube, making the glued area slightly larger than the repair patch.

Step 04

Allow the glue to go tacky then peel the backing from the repair patch and firmly press the patch, backside down, on to the glue. Ensure that the patch edges are flat and keep pressure on it for about a minute. Use the abrasive to dust some French chalk on to the repair and allow the glue to dry fully.

Step 05

Put one side of the tyre on the rim. Inflate the tube slightly and push its valve down through the rim hole. Work the whole of the tube on to the rim and under the tyre. Push the valve upwards slightly and lift the other side of the tyre over the rim. Work the rest of the tyre back on the rim. If it proves difficult, use a tyre lever to help fit the last part.

Adjusting your gears

Front mech

If your gear shifts between chainrings are slow, or if the chain gets derailed when you shift or rubs against it, the front mech needs adjusting. You do this by setting it to its optimal working position.

Step 01

Shift the chain on to the largest sprocket and smallest chainring. Undo the cable clamp bolt on the front mech.

Step 02

Screw the low (marked L) adjuster until the chain is 2mm away from the inside plate of the front-mech cage.

Step 03

Pull the cable taut and tighten the clamp bolt.

Step 04

Shift the chain on to the smallest sprocket and biggest chainring. Screw the high (H) adjuster until the outside plate is 2mm clear of the chain.

Cyclosportive_

Rear mech

If rear mech shifts are slow, or the chain jumps sprockets or becomes derailed during shifts, you need to set the rear mech up to its optimal working position.

Step 01

Shift to the big chainring and small sprocket. Undo the cable clamp.

Step 02

Adjust the high screw (H) until the chain runs quietly when you turn the pedals. Tighten the cable clamp.

Step 03

Shift gears upwards, turning the barrel adjuster to speed up slow shifts or reduce over-shifts.

Step 04

Adjust low (L) screw if the inside of the rear mech cage rubs on the spokes.

Bike maintenance workshop Q&A

Here are some troubleshooting answers to common questions concerning bike maintenance.

Q: How often should I get my bike serviced?

A: Get it fully serviced twice a year, once before the winter and again before the summer. You should also do a weekly degrease, clean and lubrication of the drive train.

Q: How do I prolong the life of the bearings on my bike?

A: Check cranks, pedals, hubs and headset for play or over-tightness. If you find any, either adjust it yourself using the instructions in a good bike-maintenance book, or take the bike to a good bike shop for some attention.

Q: How can I increase the life of my tyres?

A: Always inflate them to a pressure in accordance with the manufacturer's instructions, which are usually printed on the tyre wall. Brush off anything that might be stuck to them after each ride before it gets embedded in the tyre.

Q: Is there anything I can do to prevent punctures?

A: Use tyres with a Kevlar layer, or other brands of puncture prevention in them. Avoid riding on gravel, especially wet gravel. Look out for glass and thorns on the road. Replace worn tyres.

Q: What if my brakes become hard to apply, or won't release when I let go of the brake levers?

A: The cables are dry and worn and need replacing. Either do it yourself, as there are many good books on DIY cycle repair, or take it to a bike shop. You should replace brake and gear cables at least once a year anyway.

Q: The wheel rim catches on my brakes in the same place on each revolution.

A: Check for broken spokes, if you can't find any, the wheel has just gone out of true. Both require the attention of a bike shop.

Q: My front brake on the whole front of my bike judders, what does this mean?

A: The headset is either loose or the bearings in it are worn. This is another one for your local bike shop.

Q: My gear shifts aren't smooth, or I can't get all my gears when I shift.

A: Follow the steps for setting up you front and rear mechs on pages 136-139

Q: How do I cut down wear to the drive train?

A: Replace any worn single part before it wears out the rest: for example, a worn chain will quickly wear out sprockets and chainrings. Chains should be replaced at least every six months. If your chain jumps on a single sprocket, that sprocket could be worn and should be replaced.

Q: How do I prevent my brakes screeching or juddering when I apply them?

A: Inspect the brake blocks and remove any foreign bodies that might become embedded in them with tweezers. This cuts down on rim wear too. Clean wheel rims with solvent to remove residue that can affect brake performance. Do not get solvent on the tyre.

Q: What do I need in a home tool kit?

A: A multi-tool, crosshead screwdriver, tyre levers, puncture repair kit, long-nosed pliers, a cable cutter, a chain breaker tool and various brushes, sponges and cloths for cleaning

Q: How can I protect my frame from scratches?

A: If it hasn't got one, fit a chain-stay protector on the side where the chain runs to stop it chipping the paintwork when riding over rough surfaces. Protect places where the various cables rub against the frame with special patches that fit between the cables and frame.

Q: What should I do if the chain jumps when I pedal?

A: Degrease, clean and lubricate it. Back pedal to see if the chain runs smoothly through the rear gear mech. If there is a kink in it take hold of the chain where the kink is with both hands and gently flex it sideways. Apply more oil and let it soak in. If the jumping persists you might need a new chain and/or cassette sprockets.

Q: My pedals creak when I press hard on them.

A: Check that all bolts on your cranks and chainset are tight. If the noise persists, clean and degrease your pedals, then lubricate the retention device that retains the cleat attached to your shoes in the pedals.

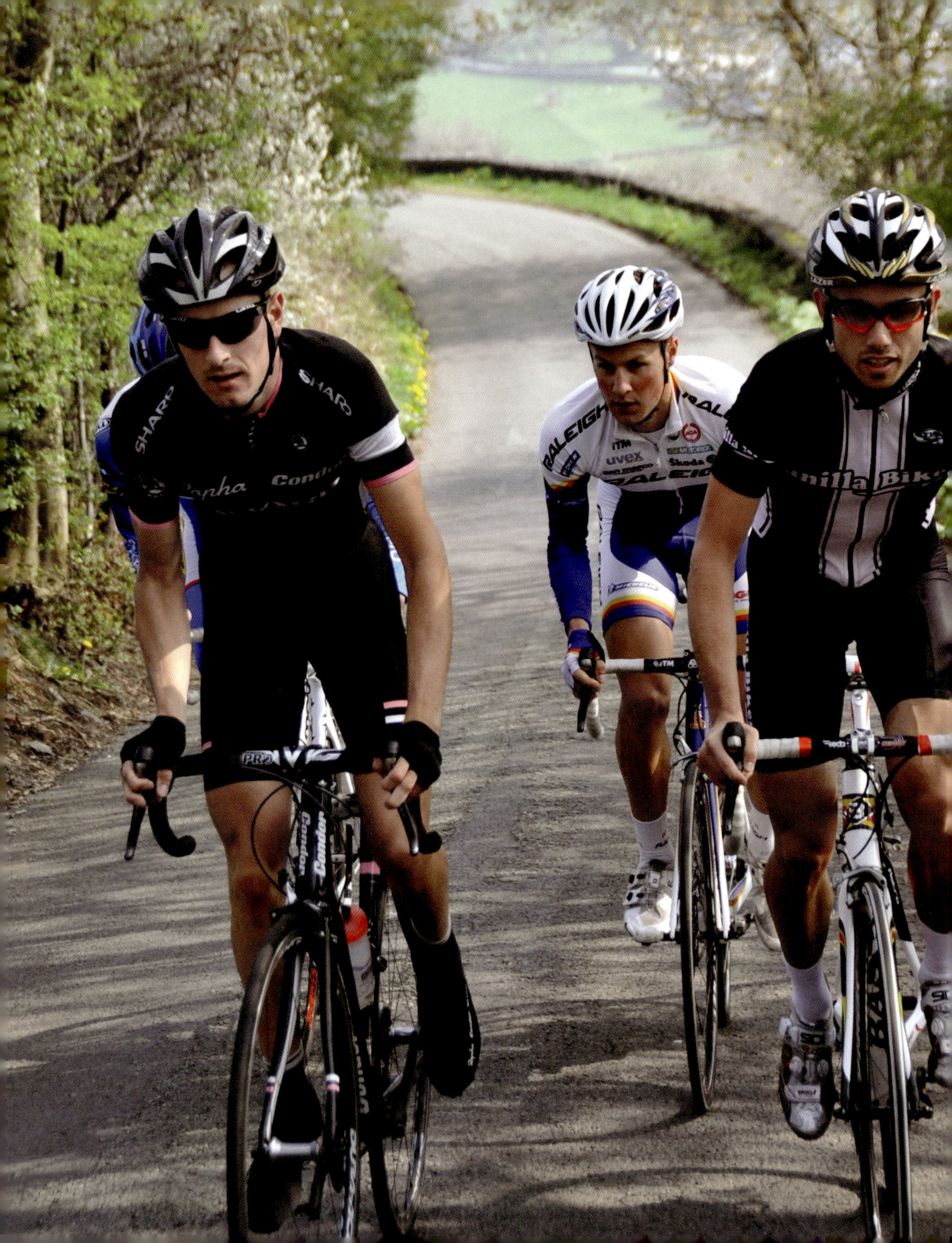
SHARP
SHARP
RALEIGH
uvex
ITM
Skoda

+ Useful References

General

British Cycling

The governing body of cycling in the UK, promoting every aspect of the sport and pastime. Their website is a huge source of cycling information. It also carries a list of most British cyclosportives. Membership includes legal support and third party insurance.

British Cycling
Stuart Street
Manchester M11 4DQ

+44 (0)161 274 2000

info@britishcycling.org.uk
www.britishcycling.org.uk

Cyclists' Touring Club

A national cyclists' organisation, the CTC has been protecting and promoting the rights of cyclists since 1878. CTC is a not-for-profit organisation that is funded through its membership and donations in return for support. They promote and encourage cyclosportives.

CTC
Parklands
Railton Rd
Guildford
Surrey GU2 9JX

+44 (0)844 736 8450;
direct line +44 (0)1483 238 337

cycling@ctc.org.uk
www.ctc.org.uk

Sportive media

Cycling Weekly

This weekly magazine carries news and reports on cyclosportive events all over the UK and abroad, and has good articles on training and technique. As well as a paper edition there is also useful website.
www.cyclingweekly.co.uk

Cycling Active

A monthly magazine reporting on and previewing British cyclosportives, and providing good articles on training and technique.
www.cyclingactive.com

Cycling Plus

A monthly magazine that covers taking part in and training for cyclosportives. It also has lots of handy stuff regarding bike mechanics and bike care.
www.cycling.magazine.co.uk

Websites

www.bikeradar.com – a website containing news, features and reviews on everything cycle related, from doing BMX tricks to the Tour de France. It contains lots of information on cyclosportives.

www.cyclosport.org – a website dedicated to cyclosportives. It carries the full UK calendar, as well as details of many other events worldwide. There are reports on sportives, articles on training and reviews of equipment.

www.roadcyclinguk.com – a website dedicated to the world of dropped handlebars with plenty of good info on cyclosportives, how to train for them and what equipment to use.

Further reading

The Bike Repair Manual, by Chris Sidwells, published by Dorling Kindersley, 2008, is a small, convenient-to-use book that gives straightforward instructions on how to repair and care for your bike.

Zinn and the Art of Road Bike Maintenance, by Lennard Zinn and Todd Telander, published by Velo Press, 2009, is a larger book dedicated just to road bikes.

The Cyclists Training Manual, by Simon Doughty, published by A&C Black, 2007, covers training for all types of bike racing. It is well worth reading if you plan to finish near the front of cyclosportives.

The Cyclists Training Bible, by Joe Friel, first published by Velopress in 1999. This book acts like a paper coach, taking the readers through step by step to plan their training. It's a little bit outdated but still a safe and sound way to train.

The big events

UK and Ireland

Etape du Dales
www.etapedudales.co.uk

Etape Hibernia
www.etapehibernia.com

Kilotogo-Verenti Series
www.kilotogo.com

Southern Sportives
www.southernsportive.com

The Dragon Ride
www.wiggledragonride.com

Wiggle Super Series
www.wiggle.co.uk

France

Etape du Tour
http://letapedutour.fr

L'Ardéchoise
http://blog.ardechoise.com

La Marmotte
www.cyclomundo.com

Italy

Felice Gimondi
www.felicegimondi.it

L'Eroica
www.eroica-ciclismo.it

Maratona dles Dolomites
www.maratona.it

Belgium

Tilf-Bastogne-Tilf
http://sport.be.msn.com/cyclingtour/tilffbastognetilff

Tour of Flanders
http://sport.be.msn.com/cyclingtour/rondevanvlaanderen/2011/eng

Holland

Amstel Gold
www.amstelgoldrace.nl

Spain

Quebrantahuesos
www.quebrantahuesos.com

America

Levi Leipheimer's King's Ridge Gran Fondo in California www.levisgranfondo.com

Team Livestrong Challenge Austin
www.livestrong.org

Travel companies

A number of travel companies provide packages that include travel, accommodation, the cost of entry and support for cyclosportives events. These include:

www.lafuga.cc
http://ronanpensectravel.com
www.sportstoursinternational.co.uk
www.pyreneespursuits.com

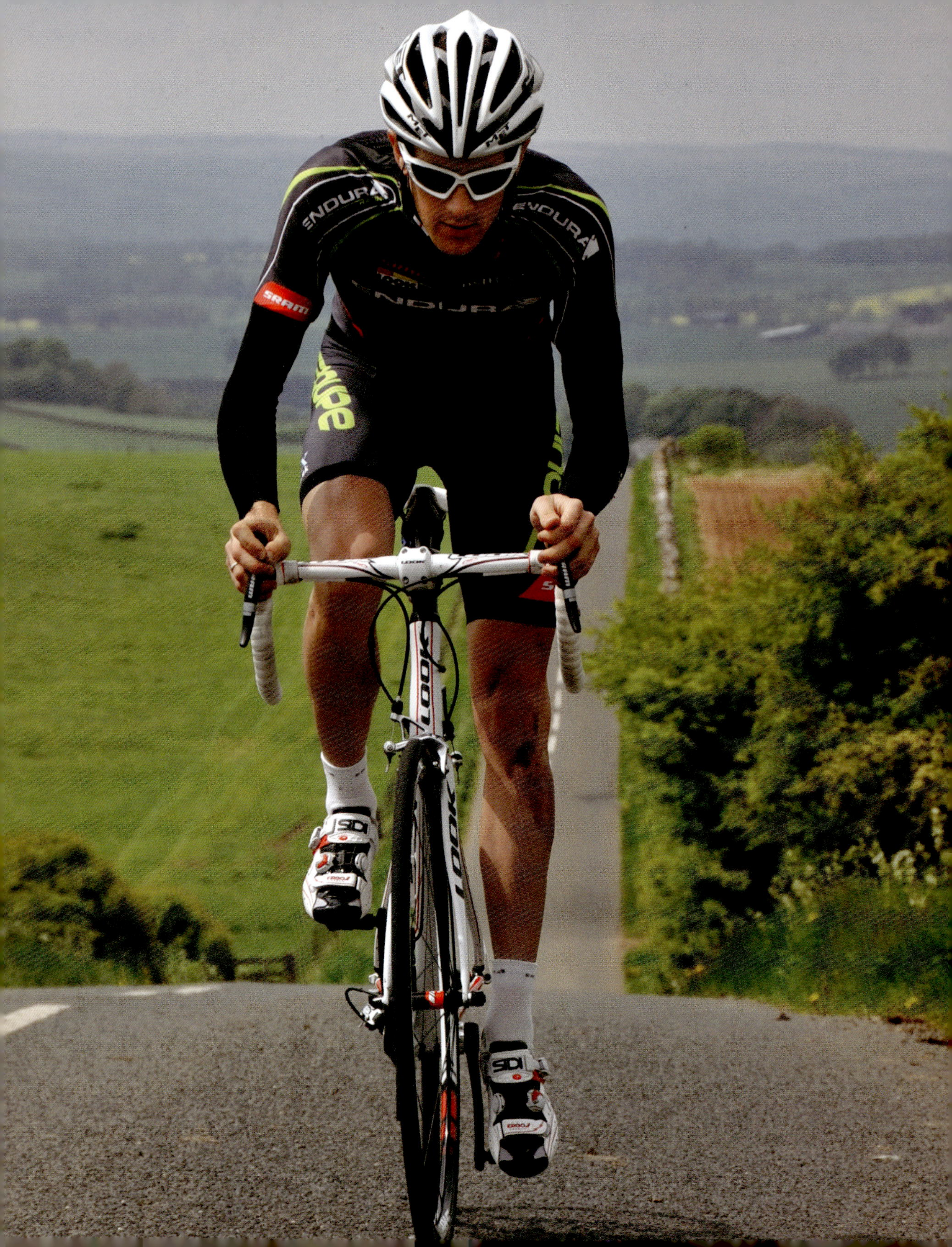
ENDURA
ENDURA
ENDURA
SRAM
LOOK
LOOK
SIDI
SIDI

+ Index

80km plan 84–5
160km plan 88–9
Amstel Gold (Holland) 16

bags, under-the-saddle 25
ball bridge exercise 92
ball crunches 90
Belgium, events in 10, 15, 157
bench presses 126
bent-over row 126
bikes 19–21
    maintenance 139–53
    materials 20
    set-up 33–7
Boardman bikes 21, 22
bonking 116
bottle cages 23–4
Bowley, Richard 62
boxer crunches 93

cadence 43, 52
cake 106, 108
carbohydrates 112, 113
case studies
    first-time participant 38
    food and drink 118
    pace judgement 42–3
    skills 62
    supplementary training 102
    training 90, 136
    weather 71
chainsets 19, 21
Chamois crème 33
checks, pre-ride 8, 142–5

chest stretches 100
cleaning 8, 22, 139–42
climbing 41, 49–52, 53, 69–70, 81, 133
clothing 8, 28–33, 70
computers 8, 25
conditioning exercises 126
Conjugated Linoleic Acid (CLA) 135
core skills 41
core strengthening 90–8, 102, 125, 126

dead lifts 125
descending 41, 56–7, 62
diary, training 80
diet, cyclosportive 116–17
Downing, Russell 54, 136
drag 28
Dragon Ride 12
Dytch, Jo 38

efficiency 43–6
endurance 65–6
energy bars 106, 107, 108
Etape du Dales (UK) 12
Etape du Tour (France) 3, 9, 11, 13, 42
events 3, 7–12, 15, 17, 62, 157
    first time 83
exercises 90–102, 125–8

fast-twitch loss 125
fat (body) 111–12
    and glucose 66, 68
fat (dietary) 114–15
Felice Gimondi (Italy) 14
finishing 9

fish oil 134
fitness 65–6, 72
    see also training
Fleeman, Dan 109
following 54
food and drink 9, 23–4, 70
    after events 111
    before the event 105–6
    training 111–18, 134
    while riding 41, 58–61, 106–9
food groups 112–16
France, events in 3, 9, 10, 11, 13, 42, 90

gears 19, 50, 148–51
gels 60, 107, 108, 109, 116
gloves 30
glucose, and fat 66, 68
glycaemic index (GI) 112–14
GPS 25–6
group riding 41, 52–6, 122–3

hamstring raises 96
hamstring stretches 100
handling, bike 41, 46–9
heart-rate
    monitors 25, 26
    test 79
helmets 30
hills 41, 49–52, 53, 69–70, 81, 133
hip stretches 101
Hoban, Barry 56
Holland, events in 16, 157
hydration 106, 107, 109, 111, 118

improving 121–6
inner tubes 23, 24, 25
interleukin-6 (IL-6) 66
Ireland, events in 136, 157
Italy, events in 9, 10, 14, 157

Kay, Alistair 42
Keegan, Ron 71
key capacities 77–8

La Marmotte (France) 9, 13, 90, 157
L'Ardéchoise (France) 13, 157
leg presses 125
L'Eroica (Italy) 14
levels, intensity 78–80, 83

lights 22, 23, 25, 26
limiters 128
lip salve 33
load-bearing exercise 126
long rides 66, 68–9, 77, 86–7, 90, 123–4
    food and drink 109
    training plans 88–9
'long-distance works' anomaly 66, 68–9

McSharry, Peta 122
maintenance, bike 139–53
management mode 9
Maratona dles Dolomites (Italy) 10, 14, 157
marginal gains 121
materials 20–1
maximum heart-rate test 78
mental challenge 71–2, 74
micro-nutrients 115–16
Millar, Robert 108
minerals 115–16
Mitchell, Nigel 105, 118
mobile phones 107
money 107
Mount Ventoux (France) 11, 42
mudguards 22, 23, 25, 27
multi-tools 23, 24

Newey, Richard 52, 74
nutrition 7

off-season 129–30
oils, body 33
on-off switches 83, 86
'one hour power' 78
one-legged flying exercises 128
one-legged squats 126, 127
one-minute intervals 130
origins of cyclosportive 1, 3

pace judgement 41–3, 69
pedalling 44–6
pedals 30
plank exercise 95
plans 128–9
    80km 84–5
    160km plan 88–9
    first-timer's 80–3
pre-ride checks 8, 142–5
protein supplements 134–5

Index

proteins 114
pumps 23, 24, 25
punctures 23, 146–7

quadriceps stretches 99
Quebrantahuesos (Spain) 16

Race Across America (RAAM) 74
recovery 111
references 155–6
registration, for events 8
rest 129
Reynolds, Hannah 90
road bikes 20
routes, familiarisation 7
running 129

set-up, bike 33–7
shorts 28, 30
shoulder fly 126
side raises 94
side to sides 98
Simpson, Mark 102
Spain, events in 10, 16, 157
speed for free 41
speed and power sessions 130, 132–4
squats 125, 126, 127
start 9
step back exercises 126–7
strength training 125–8
stretching 99–101, 102
summer, riding in 28
sunscreen 33
supplementary training 90–102
supplements 134–5
    see also micro-nutrients; minerals; vitamins
Sutton, Shane 65
sweet spot 80
Swiss balls 90

three-minute steps 133–4
Tilf-Bastogne-Tilf (Belgium) 15
time trials 133
timing transponders 8
Timmis, Adrian 33–7

Tour de France 9, 119
Tour of Flanders (Belgium) 15
training 66, 69, 130–6, 135
    80km plan 84–5
    160km plan 88–9
    diary 80
    hills 69–70
    interval 78
    key capacities 77–8
    levels of intensity 78–80
    long rides, 86-7m 90
    nutrition 111–18
    off-season 129–30
    plans 128–9
    strength 125–8
    supplementary 90–102
    and weather 70–1
travel companies 157
trunk raises 97
turbo trainers 25, 28, 130
tyre levers 23, 24, 25
tyres 23

under-the-saddle bags 25
United Kingdom, events in 12
United States, events in 9, 74, 157
upper body exercises 126
upper tempo 80
upper-back stretches 101

Van Impe, Lucien 70
Verenti Kilmeston bikes 20, 21, 22, 23
visualisation 43, 46, 53
vitamins 115–16
VO_2 max 77–8, 83, 132, 135

warming up 9
weather 33, 70–1, 129
wicking materials 28
wind chill 33
winter 129
winter riding 22–3
    clothing for 30–3

zones 78, 80

Acknowledgements

I'd like to acknowledge the help of all the coaches and cyclists who've shared their experiences to help me write this book. My particular thanks go to Jo Dytch, Richard Bowley, Richard Newey, Mark Simpson, Nigel Mitchell and Russell Downing. Thanks also go to Hannah Reynolds, Barry Hoban, Dan Fleeman, Adrian Timmis, Alistair Kay, Robert Millar and Peta McSharry.

Chris Opie deserves special mention for being such a good and patient model. As do Ricci and Liz Pascoe for lending me Bissoe Bike Hire and the Ricci Bike Chain shop in Cornwall for photo-shoots, not just in this book but for many other things I've written over the years.

Thanks to Becky Senior and Sarah Cole, and all at A&C Black for making my ideas look good. And for all the cyclists pictured in this book, and many who've helped but aren't. Finally, thanks to my wife Kathleen for her patient support and practical help in writing Cyclosportive.

ALSO AVAILABLE

Ride A Stage Of The Tour De France
9781408133330

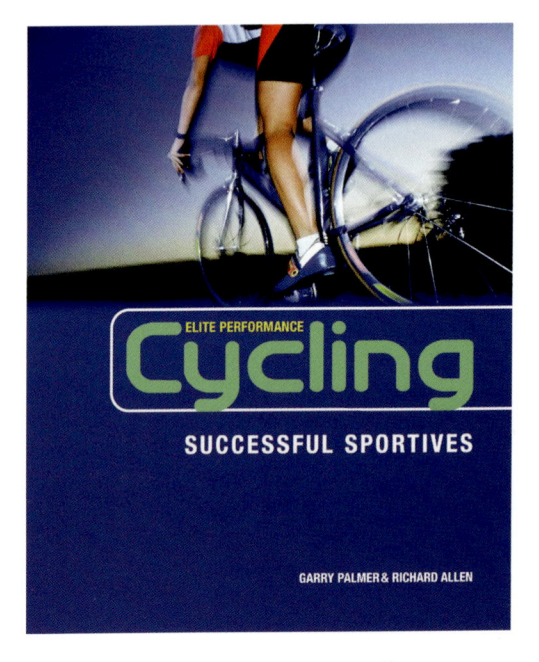

Elite Performance Cycling Successful Sportives
9781408100493

ALSO AVAILABLE

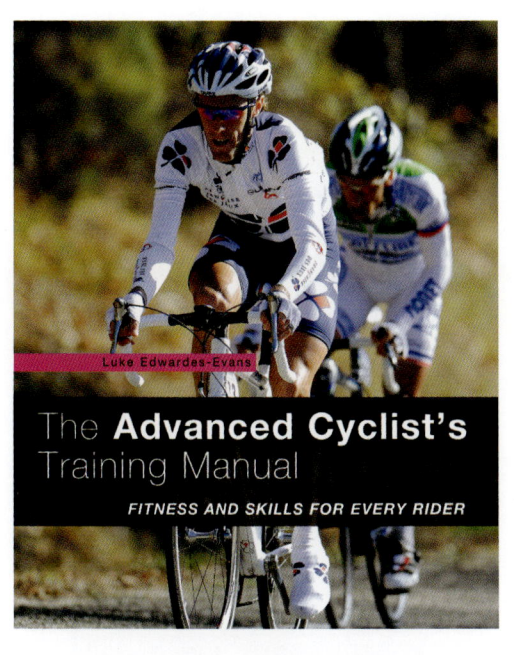

The Advanced Cyclist's Training Manual
9781408108703

The Cyclist's Training Manual
9780713677416

ALSO AVAILABLE

The Complete Guide To Endurance Training
9780713679038

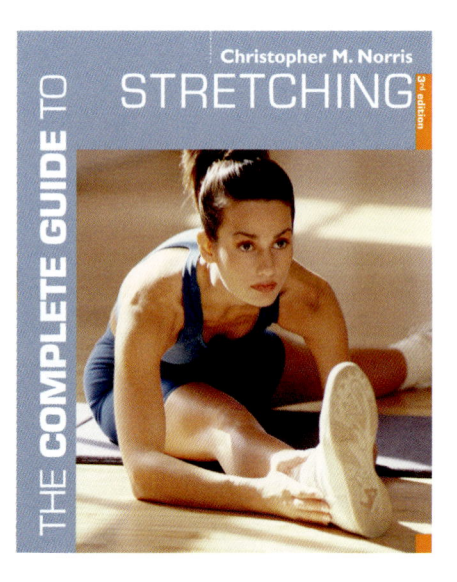

The Complete Guide To Stretching
9780713683486

The Complete Guide To Strength Training
9781408105399

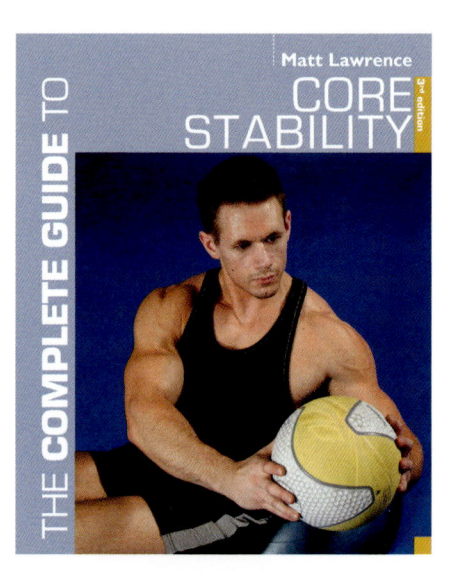

The Complete Guide To Core Stability
9781408133248

ALSO AVAILABLE

**The Complete Guide To
Sports Nutrition**
9781408105382

Sports Supplements
9780713682595

ALSO AVAILABLE

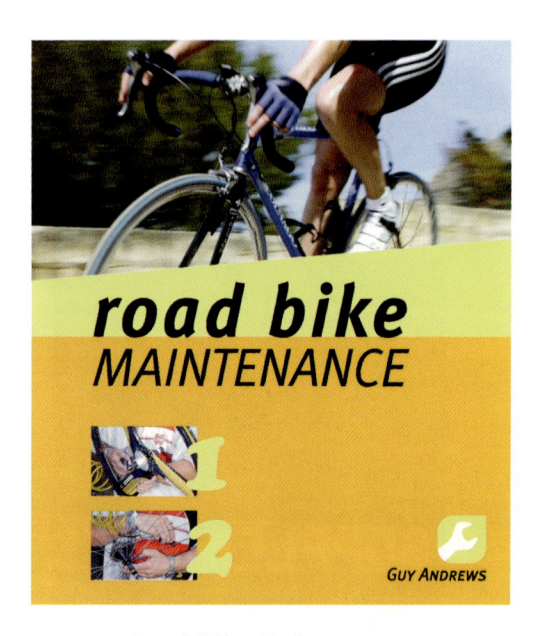

Road Bike Maintenance
9780713681994

Mountain Bike Maintenance
9780713673340

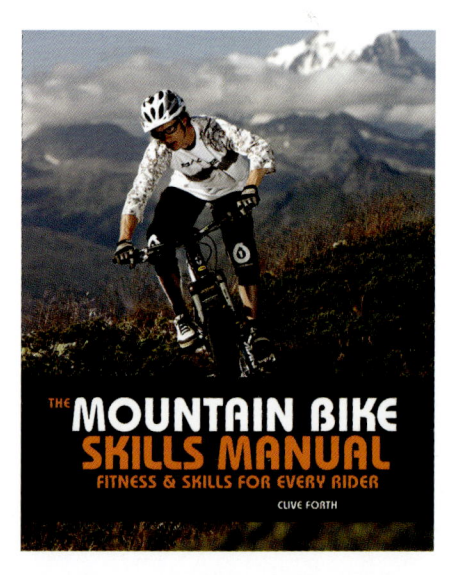

The Mountain Bike Skills Manual
9781408127322